A COMPUTER SIMULATION OF INNOVATIVE DECISION-MAKING IN ORGANIZATIONS

By

Marcia Whicker Taylor

Copyright © 1978 by

University Press of America™

division of
R.F. Publishing, Inc.
4710 Auth Place, S.E., Washington, D.C. 20023

ISBN: 0-8191-0517-1

Library of Congress Catalog Card Number: 78-56051

TABLE OF CONTENTS

PREFACE

This book utilizes computer simulation to study the amount of policy innovations adopted by organizations with varying structural characteristics. A computer model, written in Fortran IV, is developed. The computer model, which modifies the traditional rational choice model by incorporating additional assumptions about the nature of reality, is both dynamic and probabilistic.

Organizational innovation is a phenomenon worthy of significant inquiry for several reasons. First, as bureaucratic organizations thoroughly permeate our modern society, an adequate understanding of the various facets of organizational behavior becomes increasingly imperative. Secondly, the linkage between social change on the one hand and organizational innovation on the other hand, provides a rationale for studying innovation. Thirdly, the outputs of bureaucratic governmental organizations and the extent to which those outputs are innovative have a substantial impact on our lives. To date, studies of innovation in organizations have been either personal reflections and observations of individuals who have worked in governmental bureaucracies and who have observed their behavior or empirical studies with limited data bases. The innovation model is unique in that it builds a theoretical model which predicts innovative behavior in governmental bureaucratic organizations.

The innovation model assumes that sunk or fixed costs of choices, an individual's willingness to undertake calculated risks, an individual's dissatisfaction with the status quo and his or her free or unobligated resources, affect decision-making. In particular these phenomena impact upon whether the individual organizational member decides to recommend to superiors that the agency perpetuate its existing policy or adopt a policy alternative. In the innovation model, organizational members first make individual decisions in an individual processing algorithm. Then, authoritative individuals within the organization make decisions for the agency as a whole in an organizational processing algorithm. Structural features of the organization such as span of control and degree of hierarchy are varied to determine the impact of these variables on exhibited innovation.

Simulation results indicate that degree of decentralization and the nature of the choice structure an agency faces have a significant impact on the number of innovations adopted. While most types of organizations exhibit positive rates of innovation, none of the rates are very high. This indicates that the preponderance of innovation adoption occurs in an agency's youth.

ACKNOWLEDGEMENTS

Two people above all others made this book possible--Gilmer Whicker and Ola Whicker. In addition, the critical evaluation by John Wanat and the support of Folger Whicker and Terry Taylor were invaluable.

A COMPUTER SIMULATION OF INNOVATIVE
DECISION-MAKING IN ORGANIZATIONS

CHAPTER ONE

Introduction

This book investigates and analyzes organizational decision-making through the use of computer simulation. The simulation attempts to examine various organizational factors over which executives have some degree of control, and to determine which of these factors, if any, effect the rate at which an agency engages in program innovation. Within the framework of this design, organizational factors such as span of control, organizational size, age, degree of hierarchy, etc. become independent variables in the simulation while factors such as organizational resources, slack, attempted innovations, and successful innovations become dependent variables.

This book is intended to be a contribution toward a growing body of literature describing factors affecting organizational behavior. My purpose is not to examine all possible sources of organizational innovation. Indeed, there are many aspects of organizational behavior in general and organizational innovation in particular with which this model will not deal. No apologies are made for this fact, since no single presentation may deal with all human knowledge on a given subject, even when that subject is somewhat narrowly defined. In particular, in the following analysis we have intentionally omitted external forces as a cause of organizational innovation, except for the indirect impact of external factors upon organizational members' levels of dissatisfaction, since we are primarily interested in elements that can be modified by agency executives.

Rationale:

The study and understanding of organizational behavior is significant because organizations have permeated our society. An acquisition of knowledge of organization is a requisite for functioning in today's world. In his book, Modern Organization, Etzioni describes this organizational permeation of society, as well as its impact and causes. According to Etzioni, modern people spend so many of their waking hours in organizations that they have difficulty conceptualizing an alternative way of structuring social intercourse. The primary thrust toward bureaucracy and hierarchical organizations is derived from the high moral value modern society places upon rationality, effectiveness, and efficiency. Modern organizations, by creating and utilizing

1

specialization and division of labor to exploit differential talents, and chains of command to identify authority and accountability, are the most efficient forms of social groups yet known to man.[1]

In order to deal with the significance of innovation in organizations, we must first come to some agreement about the nature of innovation. Innovation is the beginning of the change process, a process of great interest to humans, due to our inherent fear of the unknown, and our desire to control our own destiny. The study of innovation is an important part of the timeless attempt by people to explain and to predict, and potentially, eventually to control all types of changes that affect themselves and their environment.

In coming to agreement about the nature of innovation, let us consider two theoretical definitions. The first definition, and no doubt the more intuitively appealing one, incorporates some notion of progress when changes occur which increase satisfaction. Using this first definition, innovation is a subset of the universal set of change. More specifically, the universal set of all alternatives which are changes from the status quo would consist of two mutually exclusive subsets--innovative changes which increase satisfaction, and non-innovative changes which do not increase satisfaction. An obvious problem with this first theoretical definition of innovation based on a notion of progress is to address the question of increases in whose satisfaction? The most simple theoretical way to derive a net change in the satisfaction level of the organization or social unit in question would be to treat the satisfaction units or utility units of each individual as being equal in weight and to sum them linearly. Should this summation prove acceptable, the operationalization and measurement of utility units would form a major obstacle to widespread use of this theoretical definition.

The second theoretical definition of innovation is less complicated than the first and does not incorporate notions of progress. It simply states that an innovation is any change from the status quo and the subset of changes which are innovations is congruent with the universal set of all changes which are changes from the status quo. The subset of non-innovative changes necessarily then becomes the null or empty set.

Which definition of innovation shall we use in our simulation of innovation in organizations? The first definition, as already mentioned, is more intuitively appealing if we are willing to assume, as are most economists, that human beings experience non-satiety in that they constantly strive to maximize their satisfaction. This "progressive" definition of innovation, however, has very real and great operationalization problems. Previously,

2

we noted that we could theoretically derive a net change in the aggregate level of satisfaction by linearly summing individual utility units. Such an assumption is based on the democratic notion of total equality which is rarely, if ever, present in organizations or social units. Hence, the assumption of democratic equality is unrealistic, even in supposedly democratic institutions.

To linearly sum utility units from different individuals, we are asserting implicitly that the units are measurable and are conducive to interval level measurement. Given the current state of social science, however, we find it difficult to measure utility. Furthermore, we cannot measure individual utility with interval scales, but rather must use ordinal rankings for each individual. Under these conditions, inter-personal utility comparisons are not possible. Similarly, the linear summation becomes meaningless.

Attempts have been made to attain interval level utility data for inter-personal utility comparisons by asking individuals how many dollars they would risk or give up to achieve a given preference.[2] However, this technique has not been employed widely enough to provide psychological preference maps of different types of individuals which we could incorporate as basic assumptions in our simulation of innovative decision-making within organizations. These problems of obtaining comparable measures of satisfaction level changes for various individuals in an organization cause us to employ the second theoretical definition of innovation here. For the purposes of this analysis, innovation and change are synonymous. Innovation, as we have operationally defined it, includes all changes from the status quo, irrespective of the impact of the change on the utility or satisfaction levels of members of the organization adopting the innovative alternative.

To return to the rationale for this study, the understanding of innovation is significant insofar as humans wish to predict their future and the rate of change from the status quo. As government bureaucrats plan to meet both clientele and political pressures, a theory of innovation would facilitate their efforts. As psychological stress and physiological disorders resulting from the fast pace of modern life increase, we as a society may need to develop a more thorough understanding of the change process, as well as its impact on human behavior and human well-being. Indeed, it may eventually become desirable to program change at a rate within the human capacity to cope with the consequent stress and disequilibrium. Any such effort by men and women to maximize their well-being and to become self-determined, insofar as they consciously decide what alternatives from the status quo are desirable and when these alternatives should be taken, must be founded on an understanding of the innovative process and of the constraints upon this process.

Man's inherent fear of uncertainty leads him to seek to understand social change, as well as organizational change. Organization innovation is related to social change, and this relationship provides an additional rationale for studying organizational innovation. Innovation can precede and cause social change, or it may be developed in response to needs created by social change. Zaltman, et al. discuss the relationship between organizational innovation on the one hand, and social change, on the other. These authors discuss a continuous and dynamic interaction between ideas, organizational practices and structure, and social change. An idea may stimulate an organizational change which, in turn, fosters innovation and change in the organization's social environment. This environmental change may ultimately create additional organizational innovation.[3]

This relationship between social change and organizational innovation provides a justification for studying the latter. Social scientists are, among other things, interested in social change. Social change may affect all parts of the political system. Change within the social environment may cause new types of demands and supports to be inputed into the political system. Social change may affect the conversion process by altering both citizen perceptions of conversion institutions and the attitudes and motivations of political actors within those institutions. By impacting upon political institutions converting demands and supports into outputs, social change may affect outputs of the political system. Social change may also affect the feedback process by coloring the way political outputs are perceived. Outputs deemed desirable to a majority prior to social change may no longer be regarded favorably; similarly, the converse may be true, with social change causing outputs once regarded as undesirable to be looked upon with favor.

Organizational change is important for a third reason--the degree to which the specific outputs of public agencies are innovative or non-innovative affects the quality of our lives. Sharkansky acknowledges this when he notes that all of us live in an "administrative state," with many of our rewards and deprivations coming from administrative agencies.[4] In addition to affecting public attitudes toward environmental policy in the long run, the degree to which the Environmental Protection Agency enforces innovative clean air standards, for example, at least partially determines the quality of air we breathe daily. Should the Interstate Commerce Commission abolish needlessly restrictive regulations on interstate transport, the prices of products we purchase which cross state lines may be lower. Whether the policies of the Office of Education are innovative or not innovative may bear upon the nature of education our children receive. Similarly, we may go through a complete list of federal agencies and determine either a direct impact or an indirect impact that

4

policies of that agency have upon our lives. Consequently, the nature of those policies--whether or not they are innovative as well as their substantive content--also affects our lives.

Nor does our discussion have to restrict itself to federal agencies. The policies of state and local governmental agencies have as great or greater impact upon the daily lives of citizens as do federal agencies. Because these policies are significant to the quality of our lives, it is imperative that sooner or later we develop an understanding of the processes whereby certain policies emerge and frequently change while other policies seem to go on indefinitely. To argue that administrative agencies are the sole determinants of policy outputs of the political and bureaucratic systems is unrealistic and is not the argument we are making here. Policy making is presumably the prerogative of the legislative branch in theory; in actuality, much policy making occurs in Congress and state legislatures. Rather, we are arguing that policy making which impinges on citizens' lives and livelihoods simultaneously occurs in administrative agencies. Sharkansky makes this point, when he notes that the work of administrative units is quite similar to the work of executives, legislators, and judges. The separate election of many executive department heads, particularly at the state and local level, as well as the appointment of regulatory heads who cannot easily be removed, create an atmosphere conducive to independent administrative policy making. Administrators are frequently the vehicle through which other branches create policy, as when they provide advice and write bills for legislators. Much legal discretion is also frequently granted administrators in carrying out their tasks.[5]

With the importance of innovation in government organizations established, let us turn to the current state of the science. Exactly how much about the development of the policies of government agencies--specifically the extent to which they are innovative or perpetuate the status quo--is known?

The State of the Science:

Writers in the field of organizational innovation may be divided into three groups of authors. The first group of authors-- Thompson, Kaufman, Mueller, Frank, Lambright, Shepard, Rowe and Boise--rely upon their experience in the field and their observations of bureaucracies to make perceptive comments about innovation. In most instances, however, these authors do not support their intuitions with empirical data. The second group of authors looking at innovation in organizations--Hage and Aiken, Mohr, Pelz and Andrews, Corwin, Helmich and Brown, Eitzen and Yetman, and Dresang--use empirical data and statistical techniques. However, their findings require further validation on a cross-section of organizations before we can legitimately accept them as

5

generalizations. The third group consists of only one author--
Slevin. Slevin essentially develops a theoretical model explaining innovation boundaries and then attempts to test the model's
implications empirically in a limited setting. A second theoretical model tangential to this third group of authors has been
developed by Cohen, March and Olsen. We will now look briefly at
the main arguments of authors in the three groups.

Thompson belongs to the first group of authors who rely primarily upon their experience in the field. Thompson argues that
bureaucratic hierarchical structure has a negative impact on
innovation, since this type of structure provides no recourse for
an individual if a superior vetoes his innovative idea. Thompson
feels that this effect comes about through the centralization of
resources in bureaucracies. Furthermore, he argues that bureaucratic organizations are politically minded, making individual
members more concerned with the internal distribution of power
and resources than the accomplishment of organizational goals.
In addition to bureaucratic structure, Thompson feels that organizational slack--a concept he does not operationally define but
describes as unused and uncommitted resources--has an impact upon
innovation. Thompson theoretically defines organizational slack
as an objective-subjective ratio where the subjectively set
aspiration level of members of the organization has been exceeded
by the objective achievement, and argues that the occurrence of
slack has a positive impact upon organizational innovation.[6]

Kaufman also belong to this first group of authors. Kaufman
argues that organizational age has a positive impact upon innovation. He contends that age is an indication of flexibility
necessary for survival, and of organizational willingness to
adopt innovations necessary to cope with environmental change.
Hence, an older organization must have acquired a successful
adaptive mechanism.[7]

Mueller presents more empirical justification of his argument than does Thompson or Kaufman by conducting a case study of
Dupont and the innovation of nylon. However, his conclusions
generalize far beyond his data base. Essentially, Mueller argues
that organizational bigness has no impact on innovation, contend-
ing that organizational bigness is the result of innovation rather
than the cause of it.[8]

Frank focuses on the impact of role-definition and job
specification on innovation. He argues that over-definition of
roles where the target performance of the role is beyond the
incumbents' means to achieve it, and under-defined roles where
the activeness and passiveness of the individuals's behavior is
ideosyncratically or culturally determined are conducive to inno-

6

vative decision-making because these roles leave the individual considerable flexibility. By contrast, well-defined roles, where the means available to incumbents are quite adequate to the performance of their roles and relations among roles are defined so as to yield a coherent and internally consistent set of roles, are not conducive to innovation.[9]

Shepard describes some innovations which help innovation resisting organizations becomes innovation producing organizations. His article is speculative in nature and provides no empirical data to back up his assertions. Shepard contends that something more basic than structural change is needed to cause an innovation impeding organization to become an innovation embracing organization. Such structural inventions are decentralization, the use of ad hoc project organizational forms, or the creation of a class of senior scientists who have freedom of mobility in the agency can help, but if the major preoccupation of members of the organization is with controlling others, with status, and with getting a larger slice of an unexpanding pie, these devices will not produce the desired results. Shepard argues that a different outlook on life, on oneself, and on others is required to produce innovative adaptability and creative application. Ultimately, Shepard suggests, we must change our methods of education, child-rearing, and organizational experience. The ideal innovator exhibits qualities of independence and autonomous inter-dependence; movement toward innovation-producing organizations require processes of personal and interpersonal re-education so that more of us develop these characteristics.[10]

Lambright sees a correlation between government involvement in research and development, on the one hand, and the rate of technological innovation, on the other hand. He notes that as government's role as society's principal supporter of R & D has grown, the rate of technological innovation has correspondingly increased. He contends that the rate of technological innovation is reduced by "professionalized" public agency resistance to innovations in their activity area which are introduced by an outsider; simultaneously, the rate of technological innovation is increased by the degree to which administrative pluralism facilitates R & D, especially in the early stages. Lambright uses weather modification as an example of dilemmas government agencies face when dealing with judgments of technological innovation. Hence, this author asserts that government financing and administrative diversity promote innovation.[11]

Rowe and Boise review current research and evolving concepts on organizational innovation. They summarize Knight's three stages of innovation at the individual level. First, an individual recognizes a problem; secondly, he initiates a search process; thirdly, he derives a problem solution innovation. Innovation takes place, according to Knight, because of the individual's desire to innovate. The innovator differs from the non-innovator in the process of identifying problems and the nature of alternatives. The non-innovator may view problems only in terms of existing problem categories and consequently may limit the solution search to known approaches. The innovator may develop new problem concepts which will subsequently generate a search for solutions not previously feasible or relevant.[12]

Drawing from the observations of James Q. Wilson, Rowe and Boise note that the very climate required to induce innovative behavior in organizations may be the same climate which will prevent its implementation. They argue that organizational diversity supports search for innovation but simultaneously increases the difficulty of obtaining a decision to innovate. Organizational designers, to the extent this is true, may have to choose between climates which induce innovative behavior and climates which are favorable to decisions on innovative proposals. A study by Evan and Black on factors associated with the success and failure of innovative staff proposals in business organizations found the following internal climate favorable to positive decisions on innovations: high professionalism of staff, formalization of the rules, communication between line and staff, the quality of proposals, the perceived need for proposals, and low professionalism of management. Organizations may need some degree of structural certainty, according to the secondary analysis of these authors, in order to act innovatively. Rowe and Boise conclude that both rational and open-ended operational climates are needed during the knowledge accumulation and diffusion stages of innovation. A loosely structured, diverse, mildy competitive psychologically secure climate operating with resources and freedom from external pressures is needed during the formulation stage, while a sufficiently rational climate is needed during the decision state to assure the quality of proposals, their orderly flow to decision-makers, and adequate communications between proposers and decision-makers. The imlementation stage of innovation, according to Boise and Rowe, generally requires a rational and efficiency-inducing organizational climate.[13]

The second group of authors employs empirical analysis and statistical tools to examine organizational innovation. Hage and Aiken, and Mohr are both authors in this second group. Hage and Aiken examine sixteen social welfare agencies over a five year period. Mohr conducts an empirical study of all full time local health departments in Illinois, Michigan, New York, and Ontario serving a jurisdiction no greater than 600,000 in population whose chief executive had held his post the entire period from 1960 to 1964. Hage and Aiken use only one meausre of innovation which is essentially the rate of program change, while Mohr uses the two measures of number of non-traditional services adopted and total number of personnel units measured in man-hours or the equivalent in dollars added in all non-traditional programs from 1960 to 1964. Both of these articles are liable to a common criticism for this type of shot-gun empirical analysis: they are atheoretical. Everything vaguely interesting and remotely related is measured in some fashion and correlated with everything else. This is not to state that the two authors do not formulate hypotheses, for both do, but when the hypotheses are either empirically supported or not supported in the process of analysis, the results are not rebound in an amended theory. Nevertheless, these two articles are pioneering insofar as they constitute early major works on innovation in organizations which are empirical in nature.

Hage and Aiken look at the impact of four categories of variables on innovation--structural variables, formalization variables, performance variables, and contextual variables. Structural variables include number of occupational specialties, amount of professional training, amount of extra-organizational professional activity, centralization, and hierarchy of authority. Their centralization score is based on the average degree of participation in the four decision-making areas of hiring personnel, promotion of personnel, adoption of new organizational policies, and adoption of new programs or services. For formalization variables, they use job codification and degree of rule observation. Using partial correlations to detemine spurious relationships, these authors find that the number of occupational specialties and degree of hierarchy have "moderate but independent relationships" with number of program innovations. The relationship with number of occupational specialties is positive and with degree of hierarchy is negative. When statistically controlled, degree of extra-organizational activity, degree of professional training, degree of rule observation, job codification, and centralization have little impact on innovation.

Hage and Aiken do not give any indication of the amount of variance of the dependent variables, which may influence their findings to some extent. Neither do they explain why they choose to control, through the use of partial correlations, structural and formalization variables, rather than any other possible combination of the four groups simultaneously. These authors find a moderate positive correlation between program change and the performance variable job satisfaction, and a moderate negative correlation with the performance variable satisfaction and expressive relations. They argue that the organizational conditions which facilitate the introduction of change, such as occupational diversity and decentralization, reduce satisfaction because of the conflicts they stimulate. Concerning contextual variables, they find a negative relationship with organizational size, no relationship with organizational auspices (whether the agency is public or private) and age of the organization, and a positive relationship with length of interaction with organizational clients.[14]

The empirical basis for Mohr's analysis of innovation in organizations is 93 local health departments. Using the number of non-traditional services adopted as a measure of innovation, he found a positive partial correlation with the chief officer's concept of scope of services which should be provided after controlling for community size, and smaller positive partials with occupational level of the community and organizational expenditures.[15] The studies of Hage and Aiken on the one hand and Mohr on the other, while utilizing data bases which superseded those of other authors, nevertheless are limited in nature. Replication of their findings is necessary to determine the extent to which their results are applicable across organizations.

Like Hage and Aiken, and Mohr, Corwin collects data from many organizations and uses statistical analysis to examine organizational innovation. Corwin identifies and compares the effectiveness of several sociological strategies of intervention used in a national effort to reform social organizations. Forty-two public schools and ten universities in the U.S. cooperating with the Teacher Corps program served as the data base. Innovativeness, the dependent variable, is ascertained through interviews and is measured by the number of new technologies introduced in the school through the Teacher Corps program. Corwin factor analyzes 35 indicators to derive seven factors explaining 51% of the variance in organizational innovation. The three factors which account for 48% of the variance are the quality and interdependence of boundary personnel (i.e. characteristics of university faculty and team leaders, including cooperation between them), organizational control exercised by the school, and the uniqueness of outside change agents. The relationship between local school control over funds and the introduction of technological innovation is negative, while the relationships between quality and interdependence of boundary personnel and technological innovation, and uniqueness of outside change agents and technological innovation are positive. Factors contributing little explanatory value are the status of the teaching staff, the quality and modernization of the context, the competence of the administration, and the professionalism and liberalism of the staff.[16]

Corwin concludes that the major dimension of the environment contributing to innovation is the amount of cooperation between the school and the university. He finds that the conflict model of change did not exist in his data base. On the basis of his analysis, Corwin offers two general hypotheses or propositions.

10

First, he contends that the way an innovation is conceived and implemented is a product of a combination of forces inside and outside the organization. Second, characteristics of occupation and organization must be taken into account to explain innovation. Corwin offers a caveat for caution because of his necessarily crude measures of complex concepts. While adhering to the caveat, we might note that many of the weaknesses inherent in the Hage and Aiken and Mohr research apply to Corwin.

Pelz and Andrews, working in a laboratory situation simulating organizational structure, found that the creative abilities of scientists and engineers who served as subjects were enhanced when these individuals worked on particular specialties as main projects for relatively short periods, and when coordination was loose. Additional factors influencing the innovative capacities of the subjects were the availability of opportunities to influence decision-makers and the availability of good methods for communicating ideas. We must be wary of the findings by Pelz and Andrews on the grounds that their analysis is a simulated organizational setting and not in a real world bureaucratic setting. However, the general thrust of their findings tend to support those of Mohr in arguing that innovation is fostered in a loosely structured professionalized organization with at least some excess resources.[17]

Helmich and Brown employ a data base from 208 chemical and allied products corporations which have experienced presidential succession at least once in a ten year period. These authors hypothesize that corporate organizations experiencing inside succession in the office of the president will exhibit less organizational change than firms undergoing outside succession. Helmich and Brown are attempting to operationalize the "new blood" concept which asserts that increases in organizational innovativeness result primarily from an influx of new personnel into authoritative decision-making positions within the organization. They control for organizational performance, the successor's style of leadership, the intensity of operations, organizational size, and administrative growth in the industry. Findings uphold the hypothesis when organizational change is measured by changes in the executive role constellation within two years after succession--i.e. the number of top personnel replaced. While this finding is interesting, Helmich and Brown have merely shown that the top executive in an industrial organizational setting tends to replace existing personnel with persons of his or her own choosing. Rather than test the "new blood" concept, they, in fact, show that the "old boy" network prevails. They do not address the questions of product, program, or policy innovations, and consequently their findings are of limited value here.[18]

Two articles tangential to this second group of authors employing empirical analysis and statistical techniques have been written by Eitzen and Yetman, and by Dresang. Eitzen and Yetman examine the effects of coaching changes on team effectiveness by using college basketball team records. While coaching changes and team effectiveness were found to be inversely related, this inverse relationship depended on team performance prior to the change, leading the authors to conclude that coaching shifts do not effect a team's winning record. Eitzen and Yetman find a curvilinear relationship between length of coach tenure and team performance. Generally, the longer the coach's tenure, the more successful the team, until a declining rate of return is reached at about 13 years.[19]

Dresang uses in depth interviews with 77 senior officials in Zambia to explore entrepreneurialism in development administration. In developing countries, departments enjoy much autonomy with a clear absence of strong and positive direction from a non-bureaucratic source of control. Dresang argues that this structural weakness in the bureaucracies of new states makes entrepreneurial behavior by officials both possible and desirable in order to maximize scarce development resources.[20] Hence, notions of structural autonomy and looseness promoting organizational innovativeness can be found in the administrative development literature, as well as the more theoretical and sociological studies of organizational behavior.

The third group of authors focus on the development of a theoretical model explaining innovative behavior. Slevin is the only author in this "group." Slevin develops a mathematical model for examining the conditions under which individuals innovate. Current success level, target success level, costs of trying new things, and rewards for successful performance are the four main model variables. Essentially a person is predicted to try something new if:

$$P_N R - C \quad P_S P \text{ and } R = (N-t)r$$

where
P_N = Probability of success with a new strategy;

P_S = Probability of success by staying with the current strategy;

R = Total possible reward over the remaining trials;

N = Total number of trials;

t = Trial number;

r = Reward per trial;

C = Costs incurred from switching to a new strategy.

Since $\quad P_N = f_1 (S,T)$

and $\quad P_S = f_2 (S,T)$

then $\quad F(S,t) = C/R$ which defines a boundary in S,T space.

The position of the individual relative to the boundary will determine whether or not he will innovate.

Having previously validated the model in a zero-cost condition, Slevin replicated the model with a cost-to-reward ratio of .25, using 84 MBA students in four classes as subjects. Participants in the validating experiment believed they were subjects of a study of decision-making under conditions of uncertainty. Prizes of free coffee and doughnuts were given to all participants and two prizes of $5.00 were given to the highest test scorers. First, each student estimated P_N. Students then essentially had the option of using up points to draw strategy cards which may or may not have resulted in higher test scores. Slevin used multiple regression on his data results to determine the shape of the P_N function.

$$P_N - P_S = C/R$$

Stepwise regression was used to determine the boundary:

$\quad .262 + .649T - S = .25$

$\qquad\qquad\qquad\qquad$ or

$\quad S = .012 + 649T$

Slevin first located individuals in a no-cost situation according to innovative predisposition and then imposed costs of innovation. The data supported the theoretical position that the imposition of costs lowered the innovation index. Slevin found a significant difference in his sample to the .01 level with a Mann-Whitney U Test. While Slevin recognizes that his validation occurs in a limited experimental setting and that he does not deal with organizations making decisions to innovate, rather than individuals doing so, he nevertheless argues that organizational innovation is a two stage process. In the first stage the individual must try something new, while in the second stage, a viable coalition must be formed for organizational implementation. Slevin contends he focusses on this first stage of individual action.[21]

There is one additional article by Cohen, March, and Olsen which is tangential to the third group of authors. Cohen, March, and Olsen have developed a decision-making model in an organizational setting under conditions of uncertainty. While their model may be applauded for more realistic initial assumptions, they do not distinguish between innovative choices and choices perpetuating the status quo. Hence, their simulation cannot be said to depict innovative decision-making in organizations.[22]

In summary, the literature on organizational innovation, while developing, is nonetheless still sparse and embryonic. The shortage of validated hypotheses about the nature and causes of organizational innovation leaves us considerable flexibility in deciding what variables to manipulate and hypotheses to test within the context of our simulation of innovative organizational decision-making.

Footnotes, Chapter One:

[1] Amitai Etzioni, Modern Organizations (Englewood Cliffs, N.J. Prentice-Hall, Inc., 1964), p. 1.

[2] Donald Stevenson Watson, Price Theory and Its Uses (Boston: Houghton Mifflin Co., 1968), pp. 124-127.

[3] Gerald Zaltman, Robert Duncan, and Johnny Holbek, Innovations and Organizations (New York: John Wiley & Sons, 1973), pp. 2-12.

[4] Ira Sharkansky, Public Administration: Policy-Making in Government Agencies (Chicago: Markham Publishing Co., 1970), p. 1.

[5] Ibid., pp. 11-12.

[6] Victor A. Thompson, Bureaucracy and Innovation (University of Alabama Press, 1969), p. 46.

[7] Herbert Kaufman, The Limits of Organizational Change (University of Alabama Press, 1971), p. 100.

[8] Willard F. Mueller, "A Case Study of Product Discovery and Innovation Costs," Southern Economic Journal, Vol. 24, No. 1 (July '57), pp. 80-81.

[9] Andrew Gender Frank, "Administrative Role Definition and Social Change," Human Organization, Vol. 22, No. 4 (Winter '63-64), pp. 240-241.

[10] Herbert A. Shepard, "Innovation-Resisting and Innovation Producing Organizations," The Journal of Business, Vol. 40, No. 4 (Oct. 1967), pp. 470-477.

[11]W. Henry Lambright, "Government and Technological Innovation: Weather Modification as a Case in Point," _Public Administration Review_, Vol. 32, No. 1 (Jan.-Feb. 1972), pp. 1-10.

[12]Lloyd A. Rowe and William B. Boise, "Organizational Innovation: Current Research and Evolving Concepts," _Public Administration Review_, Vol. 34, No. 3 (May-June 1974), p. 285.

[13]_Ibid._, p. 287.

[14]Jerald Hage and Michael Aiken, "Program Change and Organizational Properties: A Comparative Analysis," _American Journal of Sociology_, Vol. 72 (Mar. '67), p. 509.

[15]Lawrence B. Mohr, "Determinants of Innovation in Organization," _American Political Science Review_, Vol. 63, No. 1 (Mar. '69), p. 112.

[16]Ronald G. Corwin, "Strategies for Organizational Innovation: An Empirical Conclusion," _American Sociological Review_, Vol. 37, No. 4 (Aug. 1972), pp. 441-454.

[17]Rowe and Boise, p. 287.

[18]Donald L. Helmich and Warren B. Brown, "Successor Types and Organizational Change in the Corporate Enterprise," _Administrative Science Quarterly_, Vol. 17, No. 3, (Sept. 1972), pp. 371-381.

[19]D. Stanley Eitzen and Norman R. Yetman, "Managerial Change, Longevity, and Organizational Effectiveness," _Administrative Science Quarterly_, Vol. 17, No. 1 (Mar. 1972), pp. 110-116.

[20]Dennis L. Dresang, "Entrepreneurialism and Development Administration," _Administrative Science Quarterly_, Vol. 18, No. 1 (Mar. 1973), pp. 76-85.

[21]Dennis P. Slevin, "The Innovation Boundary: A Replication with Increased Costs," _Administrative Science Quarterly_, Vol. 18, No. 1 (Mar. 1973), pp. 74-75.

[22]Michael D. Cohen, James G. March, and Johan P. Olsen, "A Garbage Can Model of Organizational Choice," _Administrative Science Quarterly_, Vol. 17 (Mar. 1972), pp. 1-25.

15

CHAPTER TWO

A More Realistic Model of Innovative
Decision-Making in Organizations

The purpose of this book is to develop an innovative
decision-making model applicable in an organizational context
which takes into account criticisms of the rational choice model.
To do this, we shall briefly explain the rational choice model.
Then we shall develop an individual decision-making model which
incorporates assumptions not usually included in the traditional
rational choice model so that our model more closely approximates
reality. Hence, we are not rejecting the traditional rational
choice model, but are merely elaborating and expanding its underlying assumptions. Finally, we shall examine the impact of
various organizational phenomena upon this process.

We shall treat the individual as the basic component of the
social unit, even though our ultimate dependent variable is organizational innovation. Essentially, we will be aggregating
individual decisions to determine "organizational decisions."
While various organizational variables, including task forces and
committees, may effect the decision-making process, the individual
remains the basic decision-making unit. Hence, we must develop
some decision criteria for the individual who is faced with the
choice of whether to innovate or to perpetuate the status quo.
Since rationality has traditionally been the decision criterion
for many social science models and has gained fairly wide spread
acceptance, we shall examine that standard here.[1]

The Traditional Model:

The traditional rational choice model asserts that the
rational individual, as all individuals are said to be on some
level of understanding and interaction, seeks to maximize his own
satisfaction.[2] To do this, he looks at all possible alternatives
in any given decision situation, calculates the benefit-cost
ratio of each alternative, and chooses the alternative with the
highest ratio. Applications and modifications of the rational
choice decision criterion are found in several social sciences.[3]
Due to the difficulty mentioned earlier of comparing interpersonal
utility, satisfaction is frequently equated with money.

Economists, for example, assume that the individual firm will
seek to maximize profits, as will stockholders and entrepreneurs,
and have built an elaborate theory of income flows within the
economy based on this assumption.[4] Political scientists also
assume somewhat more implicitly that income maximization underlies

17

the decision-making of citizen participants making demands on the political system and have used this to explain the greater vigor and effectiveness of producer interests as compared to consumer interests.[5] When policies affecting a specific area of commercial enterprise are being debated, the outcome will have a great impact on the maximization process of producer interests; hence, it is "rational" for the affected producers to devote substantial resources to modify the outcome to their benefit. By contrast, consumer interests are fragmented, not only among large numbers of individuals but also within individuals; attempts to affect policy outcomes are similarly diversified. If the individual consumer is satisfaction maximizing, it is not "rational" to devote large amounts of resources to attempts to affect any one policy outcome.

A third example of the use of the assumption of rationality as a decision criterion may be found in the literature of business administration. Business administration theorists assume organizational managers will be rational in maximizing their goals.[6] Unlike economists, they do not assume a single goal but acknowledge the probability of several competing goals, and have developed the techniques of linear programming, operations research, and systems management to facilitate the application of the maximizing axiom under these conditions.[7]

Psychoanalysts, while not rejecting rationality as an organizing force for human beings, point out that significant experiences and traumatic events in an individual's background or upbringing may impact on that individual's perception of reality.[8] In order to understand how the rationality criterion is being applied to decisions, one must first understand how these traumatizing events have affected perceptions. Behavioral psychologists are strong advocates of the rationality assumption and employ it to modify behavior.[9] These social scientists contend that the individual will rationally maximize rewards and minimize penalties. To change behavior patterns, the intervener should consistently reward desirable behavior and penalize undesirable behavior.

Limitations of the Traditional Model:

Critics of the traditional rational choice model have contended that this model, while partially depicting the individual's actions and thought processes with some degree of accuracy, is nonetheless too simplified to depict real world decision-making. Two main criticisms may be levied at the traditional rational choice model on this ground.

The first criticism comes form Lindblom. Contrasting what he considers the ideal or rational choice approach to decision-

18

making where admininstrators look at the myriad of possible
alternatives in the root method with what he considers to be the
pragmatic or practical approach where they look at only a few
alternatives in the branch method, he attacks the former by con-
tending that men and women do not have the intellectual capacity
or resources to look at all alternatives in a complex problem
situation. In light of this inherent limitation on human intellect, Lindblom laments the formalization of the root approach in
the decision-making, policy formulation, planning, and public
administration literature.[10]

The traditional rational choice approach is characterized by
clarity of objectives, explicitness of evaluation, a high degree
of comprehensiveness of overview, quantification of values for
mathematical analysis whenever possible, emphasis upon finding the
best means to achieve the desired ends, and dependency upon theory.
With the successive listed comparisons or the branch approach pro-
posed by Lindblom, the "selection of value goals and empirical
analysis of the needed action are not distinct from one another
but are closely intertwined."[11] There are several consequences of
this intertwining of value goals and empirical analysis. Means-
ends analysis is often inappropriate or of limited value. The
significance of and reliance upon theory is greatly reduced or
abolished. The test of goodness of a policy is not the highest
benefit-cost ratio, but whether experts in the field agree upon
it without necessarily agreeing that it is the most appropriate
means to achieve a consensual goal.

Two crucial aspects of the branch method are this intertwining
of evaluation and empirical analysis and the tendency of the
administrator to look primarily at marginal or incremental values.
Since progression through a succession of incremental values allows
the administator to avoid permanent mistakes, and since we do not
have adequate theories in many policy areas, Lindblom proffers the
branch method as a systematic alternative to theory. Even though
the branch method is not perfect, Lindblom believes that it is
superior to the root method. Both methods exclude factors impacting upon policy, but in the branch method exclusions are deliberate,
systematic, and consequently not defensible by any existing argument. Lindblom argues that while the root method ideally does not
exclude factors, in practice it must and does.[12]

Unfortunately, Lindblom poses the two approaches as an either-
or situation--either one must follow the root method or one must
follow the branch method. Since, he reasons, one is doomed to
failure if one pursues the rational choice approach, then one
should pursue the incremental approach. Seemingly, Lindblom has
created a straw man to attack with his description of the traditional rational choice model; as previously noted, the only

19

"theory" on which this model is founded is that of rational maximization of satisfaction, to the extent satisfaction is represented by accumulated resources units. Nonetheless, Lindblom's criticism of the limited capacity of human intellect is valid and we shall incorporate it into our innovative decision-making model by limiting the number of alternatives available to the individual in any given decision situation.

Etzioni, recognizing the dilemma created by Lindblom's either-or situation, argues for mixed scanning as a third approach to decision-making.[13] There are two features to mixed scanning: high-order fundamental policy-making processes which set basic directions for bureaus on the one hand, and incremental policy-making decisions which prepare for fundamental decisions and implement concluded fundamental decisions on the other. Etzioni argues that an advantage of mixed scanning is that it provides a strategy for evaluation but does not include hidden structural assumptions. Because utilizing different scanning levels is flexible, it is especially adapted for environments of varying stability and by actors with varying degrees of control and consensus-building capabilities. While Etzioni's theoretical argument is appealing, he provides no attempts at operationalizing his method and gives few examples. He is not explicit about the data needs of actors and the periods of time required for fundamental decisions. Neither does he elaborate how incremental decisions in mixed scanning will work toward fundamental decisions or be any less conservative or status quo oriented than incremental decisions in the branch approach. Unfortunately, Etzioni does not talk about the innovation costs of changing fundamental policies and the concommitant agency resistance to incurring such costs.

The second major criticism of the traditional rational choice model comes from March and Simon who emphasize the concept of initiation. They criticize theories of rational choice for failing to distinguish between the continuation of an existing program of action and change in the program. (As we noted, this criticism may also apply to mixed scanning.) Rational choice models consider only that the decision-maker has two or more alternatives and that he must determine the better or best. March and Simon argue that the effect of sunk costs and innovation costs--two items not considered by traditional rational choice models--is to produce program continuity.[14]

March and Simon claim that individuals give preferred treatment to alternatives representing continuation. One reason for this preference for continuity lies in the fact that the individual does not consider alternatives to continuity until he has reached a certain degree of dissatisfaction with the present course of action. The amount of search for a new approach increases as satisfaction with the past approach decreases. While

20

ganizational variables such as degree of hierarchy and span of
ntrol upon the individual decision process when the individual
faced with choosing between innovation and lack of innovation.
timately we hope to logically confirm hypotheses concerning the
lationship between internal organizational control variables
d organizational decisions to pursue policy innovation. First,
wever, let us look more closely at the nature of simulation and
delling, so that we understand the strengths and limitations of
e methodological technique we employ.

ootnotes, Chapter Two:

[1]Chris Argyris, "Some Limits of Rational Man Organizational
eory," Public Administration Review, Vol. 33, No. 3, (May-June
973), pp. 253-267.

[2]Charles E. Lindblom, "The Science of Muddling Through,"
ublic Administration Review, Vol. 29, (Spring 1959), pp. 1-86.

[3]Argyris.

[4]Paul Samuelson, Economics: An Introductory Analysis (New
ork: McGraw-Hill, Inc., 1967), pp. 474-482.

[5]Grant McConnell, Private Power and American Democracy (New
ork: Alfred A. Knopf, 1966), pp. 11-29.

[6]R. E. Marsten, W. W. Hogan, and J. W. Blankenship, "The
oxstep Method for Large-Scale Optimization," Operations Research,
ol. 23, No. 3 (May-June, 1975), pp. 389-405.

[7]Numerous articles in the business literature illustrate
this point including the following:

W. D. Cook, M. J. L. Kirby, and S. L. Mehndiretta, "A
Linear Fractional Max-Min Problem," Operations Research, Vol. 23,
No. 3 (May-June 1975), pp. 511-512. This article deals with a
generalized case of the fractionalized max-min problem prevalent
in the literature which is equivalent to a quasi-convex programming
problem whose optimal solution lies at the vortex of the feasible
region.

Graham McMahon and Michael Florian, "On Scheduling with Ready
Times and Due Dates to Minimize Maximum Lateness," Operations
Research, Vol. 23, No. 3 (May-June 1975), pp. 475-482. These
authors develop a brancy-and-bound method to sequence jobs on a
single processor in order to minimize maximum lateness, subject
to ready times and due dates. An unusual feature of this method

most theories of choice have not distinguished between the alternative of continuing and alternatives of change, these authors
contend that an adequate theory of innovation would not treat the
two symmetrically. The alternative of continuing must be differ-
entiated from alternatives of change by coupling the latter with
a theory of search for new alternatives.[15] Hence, the main argument of Simon and March is that innovative alternatives should be
treated differently from the status quo in a rational choice
model. From these hypotheses of these authors, we shall incorporate sunk costs, innovation or search costs, and dissatisfaction
with the status quo as a motivation to search out alternatives to
the status quo into our innovative decision-making model.

An additional concept incorporated into our decision-making
model is that of non-decisions. Non-decisions have long been
recognized by political scientists as having an impact on policy
outcomes.[16] In effect, a non-decision is a decision to do nothing,
or in this case, a decision to avoid innovative actions and to
perpetuate the status quo. The concept of non-decisions implicitly
recognizes the significance of time in a decision-making model.
In any given time period, decisions and non-decisions occur--that
is, decisions to innovate and decisions to perpetuate the status
quo take place. To simplify matters, our model here will establish
a one-to-one equivalency between time periods and decision-making
periods. In twenty time periods, for example, an individual can
make and does make twenty decisions. Each of the twenty may be
a "real" decison in that the individual chooses to pursue an
innovative alternative, or it may be a "non-decision" in that he
chooses to do nothing and to therefore perpetuate the status quo.

Bachrach and Baratz delineate four types of non-decison-
making: invocation of force to prevent demands for change; use
of power to make threats of sanctions against initiators of
potentially threatening demands; invocation of an existing bias
in the political system such as a norm, precedent, rule, or procedure to prevent a demand for change; and reshaping or strenghen-
ing the mobilization of bias to block change demands. A fifth
situation similar to non-decision-making will more closely
resemble that of our model, for the rules or procedures of chain
of command and hierarchial flow of decisions may be invoked by a
risk-averting superior to ignore the demands or suggestions of
his subordinates for innovation.

The Innovation Simulation Model:

The primary concepts underlying this innovation model are not
original to this author. The originality of this book lies in the
author's development of a dynamic probabilistic simulation model,
and the utilization of this to logically confirm or fail to confirm hypotheses concerning the impact of organizational variables

on decision-making within bureaucratic organizations. Specifically, we shall generate hypotheses concerning two major dependent variables: one is the total number of organizational decisions made where the status quo is rejected in favor of an innovative alternative; the second is the rate of cumulative innovation change over a specified time period. We shall distinguish between an individual decision and an organizational decision. The model presupposes that every individual in the organization is capable of making decisions between perpetuating the status quo and choosing an innovative alternative which may be passed upward to his or her superior, and in fact does so. However, only certain individuals have the authority to make organizational decisions--that is, decisions in which the organization commits resources in hopes of securing some gain. The number of authoritative individuals who can make organizational decisions is one of the organizational variables to be tested in the model.

Our innovation model modifies the traditional rational choice model within an organizational context to achieve greater conformity with reality. From the rational choice model we adopt the assumptions of satisfaction maximization which is approximated by resource maximization, as well as benefit-cost analysis to determine priorities among policy alternatives. Recognizing that resources are the best easily measured surrogate of satisfaction, economists have adopted this technique of equating utility maximization with income maximization for both individuals and organizations.[17] Downs also argues that bureaus have an inherent tendency to expand; since organizations cannot expand without resources, they seek to maximize resource units at their disposal.[18] Unlike the traditional rational choice model, we shall make five additional assumptions both to take into account criticisms of the traditional model and to make our basic model assumptions more realistic.

The first new assumption of our innovative decision-making model or expanded rational choice model is to recognize the limitations of human intellect by limiting the number of alternatives potentially available to an individual in any given decision situation. We assume that the number of alternatives potentially available to any individual in any decision situation is not unlimited, but rather is limited by both the individual's inherent intellectual capacity to grasp and deal with different alternatives at any point in time and by the degree to which innovative alternatives to the status quo have been discovered and promulgated in any given policy area.

The second new assumption is derived from March and Simon; we assume that the number of alternatives available to an individual in any given decision situation is not a given, but is a function of the motivation of the individual to search them out,

as well as a function of his or her ability to eng[ ] search activities. Motivation to search out innov[ ] tives is directly related to the individual's diss[ ] the status quo; the ability to search for innovati[ ] is directly related to the resources an individual[ ] her disposal which have been allocated for this pu[ ] at least have not been allocated for another purpo[ ]

The third new assumption is to recognize that[ ] paribus, sunk or fixed costs bias the decision-make[ ] status quo. This assumption of sunk costs is widel[ ] by both economists and accountants, as well as poli[ ] are unwilling to choose innovative alternatives in[ ] a war or to discontinue the development of a sophis[ ] sive weapons system because of previously sunk inve[ ] we shall refer to sunk or fixed costs to mean expen[ ] assets which can be used only if the status quo is [ ] and which must be discarded or lost if an innovativ[ ] is selected.

The fourth new assumption of our model of inno[ ] making is to acknowledge that the payoff from any i[ ] native is not absolutely certain prior to engaging [ ] tive, but rather contains a certain element of risk.[ ] innovative alternative contains a certain amount of [ ] the risk may vary from a great deal to very little i[ ] accepted by business managers, public administrators[ ] consultants, and political advisors. Two techniques[ ] minimize risks associated with innovative alternativ[ ] development of contingency plans and diversification[ ]

The fifth new assumption is that individuals va[ ] willingness to take risks. This assumption that indi[ ] varying degrees of willingness to take risks has been[ ] verified by David McClelland in his work on entrepren[ ] need achievement.[19] McClelland found that entreprene[ ] greater willingness to take moderate risks than did p[ ] suing other occupations, and that approximately fifty[ ] a large number of these persons appeared in a country[ ] able spurt of economic growth and development occurre[ ]

Armed with these additional assumptions which ha[ ] our traditional rational choice model into one which m[ ] rately reflects the process whereby an individual deci[ ] pursue policy innovation or to reject it in favor of p[ ] the status quo, we shall establish a more detailed alg[ ] depicting this individual decision-making process. Th[ ] look at how the decisions of individuals are passed th[ ] hierarchical organization, at how individual decisions[ ] translated into organizational decisions, and at the e[ ]

is that a complete solution is associated with each mode of the enumeration tree.

H. J. Zimmerman and M. A. Pollatschek, "The Probability Distribution Function of the Optimum of a 0-1 Linear Program with Randomly Distributed Coefficients of the Objective Function and the Right-Hand Side," Operations Research, Vol. 23, No. 1 (Jan-Feb. 1975), pp. 137-149. A refinement of linear programming, this article focuses on problems with stochastic price vectors and the stochastic right-hand side of the system of constraints.

[8]Hanse H. Strupp, "Patient-Doctor Relationships: Psychotherapist in the Therapeutic Process," Experimental Foundations of Clinical Psychology, ed. Arthur J. Bachrach (New York: Basic Books, Inc. 1962), pp. 576-613.

[9]Murray Sidman, "Operant Techniques," Experimental Foundation of Clinical Psychology, ed. Arthur J. Bachrach (New York: Basic Books, Inc. 1962), pp. 170-210. Sidman argues that one of the most relevant contributions of experimental psychology to clinical psychology has been the contributions made by operant conditioning to behavioral manipulation.

[10]Lindblom, p. 80.

[11]Ibid.

[12]Ibid., p. 86.

[13]Amitai Etzioni, "Mixed Scanning: A Third Approach to Decision-Making," Public Administration Review, Vol. 27, No. 5 (Dec. 1967), pp. 385-392.

[14]James G. March and Herbert A. Simon, Organizations (New York: John Wiley and Sons, Inc., 1958), p. 173.

[15]Ibid., p. 174.

[16]Peter Bachrach and Morton S. Baratz, Power and Poverty: Theory and Practice (New York: Oxford University Press, 1970), pp. 220-221.

[17]Donald Stevenson Watson, Price Theory and Its Uses (Boston: Houghton Mifflin Co., 1968), pp. 124-127. Economists continue, for the purpose of simplicity, to equate utility units and resource units on a one-to-one basis, despite a recognition that the marginal utility of money declines as total resources increase.

[18]Anthony Downs, _Inside Bureaucracy_ (Boston: Little, Brown and Company, 1967), pp. 257-258.

[19]David C. McClelland, _The Achievement Motive_ (New York: Appleton-Century-Crofts, Inc., 1953).

David C. McClelland, _The Achieving Society_ (Princeton, N.J.: D. Van Nostrand Co., Inc., 1961).

CHAPTER THREE

The Virtues and Vices of Computer Simulation

In the previous chapter, a formal theory of innovative
decision-making in organizations was discussed. In this chapter,
we shall consider an appropriate methodology to present this
theory and to examine its logical implications. Essentially,
there are three options. We might present the theory of innovation verbally and employ verbal reasoning to deduce logical consequences of the theory. We might develop mathematical equations
describing the functional relationships between components of the
innovational theory and then attempt to determine the consequences
of the theory by solving the equation system. A third option
would entail the development of a computer model incorporating
major variables and relationships in the innovation theory; the
logical consequences of the innovation theory would then be
determined by using the innovation model to simulate various
input conditions. We shall discuss each of these three options
in greater detail.

Verbal reasoning is a tool of everyday living as well as the
social science research. Whitney describes the steps involved in
reflective thinking and verbal reasoning. The first step is the
occurrence of a felt difficulty which may be caused by the lack
of adaptation of means to a specified end, a need to identify the
character of an object, or a need to explain an unexpected event.
The second step involves the definition of the difficulty in terms
of a problem statement. In steps three and four, an explanation
or possible solution is suggested and then the idea is upheld by
citing supporting cases, or disproved by citing cases which refute
the suggested solution.[1]

Verbal reasoning is not a sufficient research methodology to
explore the consequences of the innovation theory. Verbal reasoning is most applicable to non-complex unidimensional problems
where the mind can keep track of the impacts of and changes in
various factors of interest. The innovation theory is neither
non-complex nor unidimensional. Verbal reasoning requires the
researcher to intuitively pick a solution to the problem at hand.
Much of the organizational literature is either silent or con-
flictual in indicating the impact of organizational structure on
innovativeness. Verbal reasoning is not adaptable to quantitative
methods and therefore fails frequently to express magnitudes of
significant relationships. Magnitudes would be of interest to us
in analyzing the consequences of the innovation theory. Unless
cases of every variant of interest can be found, verbal reasoning
does not allow for controlling for extraneous and confounding

factors. Since the innovation theory is complex, we are interested in achieving such controls. Finally, the conclusions of
verbal reasoning rest on a few cases. We might find the small
universe of cases limiting in making conclusions about the implications of the innovation theory.

A second option for exploring the consequences of the innovation theory is to employ mathematical equations. Chiang
describes the types of equations which may be used. A defini-
tional equation sets up an identity between two alternative
expressions that have exactly the same meaning. A behavior equation specifies the manner in which a variable behaves in response
to changes in other variables. Equilibrium conditions may be
specified in the third type of equation. This type of equation
has relevance only if the theory of interest involves notions of
equilibrium.[2]

Mathematical analysis is more difficult for the innovation
theory, due to the uncertainty interjected into innovation theory
analysis by the human element of decision-making. The analysis
of complex, dynamic, social behavior by means of mathematics is
difficult. The equations that describe physical system behavior
responding to simple forces often become intractable when applied
to non-physical systems. In social systems where system changes
are the result of human decision-making, it is often difficult to
even describe behavior in terms of equation, much less to obtain
satisfactory mathematical solutions. Under these conditions,
simulation becomes an alternative to the rigor and inflexibility
of mathematics on the one hand, and to the laxity and non-speci-
ficity of verbal description on the other hand.[3]

Computer simulation modelling represents the intersection of
three research tools or approaches available to the social scientist: system simulation, modelling, and use of the digital computer as a research aid. There are three types of simulation.
Person-person simulation involves interaction between two or more
people in a simulated laboratory environment. Person-machine
simulation involves interaction between a dynamic computer program
and a person responding to computer output, with the individual's
responses influencing future computer output. Machine simulation
is computer simulation, where input is fed into the computer and
modified by decision rules or criteria specified in the program.

Similarly, models as a research approach are not limited to
computer models, but may occur in many forms. Physical models
are a scaled down physical replica of the system being studied.
Schematic models include diagrams, maps, and charts of the system;
flow charts usually developed prior to computer simulation represent a type of schematic model. Symbolic models are based on
mathematics or computer code.[4]

The digital computer can be used as a research aid in several ways, one of which is simulation. Other uses of the computer as a research tool include sorting data into categories, searching through data for items meeting certain specifications, arithmetic and mathematical operations, and statistical analysis. Whereas the set of problems where these additional uses of the computer may be applied is somewhat restricted, any system which can be described in logical terms can be simulated with as much detail as is desirable being included in the model, since it is not necessary to make simplifications in order to obtain a solution as is often the case in mathematical applications.[5] Once a computer simulation model is developed, many trial runs of the system can be conducted to determine the effect of alternative assumptions, input, or system designs.

According to Schecter, social sciences have been influenced significantly by the development and use of computer simulation techniques. Declaring the impact of simulation methods upon the social sciences to be profound, Schechter identifies the tool's primary advantage as offering the social scientist the opportunity to investigate the properties of large-scale complex systems which have qualitative as well as quantitative relationships, nonlinearities, uncertainties, and ill-defined structures.[6] With the success of computer simulation techniques in the social sciences in mind, we shall look at more details of this third option for exploring the consequences of the innovation theory.

To simulate is to copy the behavior of the system under study. Fishman defines a system as "a collection of related entities, each characterized by attributes that may themselves be related."[7] According to Fishman, three features are universal to all systems: boundaries, environment, and subsystems. Two elements which describe a system state in time are magnitude and delay.[8] To simulate a system we would assume some initial state or condition for the system being studied. Next, the relations among components of the system would be quantitatively expressed. Then we would use whatever laws or rules of change we have in order to evaluate the states or positions through which the system advances over some stipulated period. By proceeding thusly, we can avoid the use of strictly mathematical analysis, or strictly verbal reasoning.[9]

Computer simulation is the use of programming statements to represent a dynamic model of a system. Maisel and Gnuglino define computer simulation as a numerical technique for conducting experiments on a digital computer. Computer simulation uses certain types of mathematical and logical models to examine physical, chemical, political, social, economic, business, and biological systems across time.[10]

The development of a number of higher-level computer languages which can be applied to system simulation have provided a means of analyzing system problems which previously could not be satisfactorily expressed by scale models, mathematical models, dynamic analogs, and other continuous behavior techniques.[11] When a computer is programmed for simulation, the machine appears to copy the real-life system. Referring not to an entity that physically resembles the real-life system but rather to a set of variables representing the principle features of the real-life system and a set of computer instructions representing the laws or decision rules that determine how these features are modified as time progresses, we say that we have a model of the real system in the computer.[12]

Reitman further describes the nature of a computer model and argues that its main purpose is prediction. A model of a system is developed by defining the rules and relationships which describe it. The model becomes the algorithm, or the statement of the problem. The simulation is the use of the model under specific and varying conditions. Prediction of system behavior is the primary purpose of simulation.[13]

Fishman contends that building a model is the first step in studying a system. A model can be formal representation of theory, a formal account of empirical observation, or a combination of both. Fishman sees multiple purposes or models. Models enable an investigator to organize his or her theoretical beliefs and empirical observations about a system and to deduce the logical implications of this organization. They lead to improved system understanding, bring the need for detail and relevance into perspective, and expedite the rate of analysis. Additional purposes of models include providing a framework for testing the desirability of system modifications, and permitting control over more sources of variation than direct study of a system would allow. Generally, models are easier to manipulate than the replicated system, and are less costly to manipulate than the real world system.[14]

Computer simulation models are used to evaluate alternatives. Fishman distinguishes between three variations of the evaluation or alternatives. First, alternatives may be evaluated through straight-forward analysis; the researcher simply specifies the input of the system and measures the output. Secondly, the researcher may evaluate the desirability of alternative system designs when the input is given and certain desirable characteristics for the output are specified. Thirdly, the researcher may be concerned about system control. In this type of analysis, the researcher specifies a system and wishes to determine the input that produces a desired output. He or she tests a non-feedback or open loop system versus a closed loop or feedback system to determine which system better augments the desired output.[15]

Discrete event digital computer simulation is now in its
third decade of existence. This technique can be used to study
such diverse problems as the turtle population on the Australian
Great Barrier Reef and the conflict resolution occurring between
nations. Success of this technique depends on the user's famil-
iarity with simulation modelling concepts, the programming
options available, and statistical techniques needed to produce
desired input behavior and analyze output behavior.[16] Briefly,
let us look at how social scientists have employed computer
simulation techniques.

Several simulations of systemic effects impacting on population dynamics have been developed by sociologists. Kunstadter
simulated population changes in developing countries, using
Monte-Carlo techniques to determine births and deaths, and
marriage rules to determine matrimonial couplings. Interestingly,
Kunstadter assumes a great deal of intra-family marriage. Gilbert
and Hammel simulate the same problem using a different set of
assumptions; they assume an incest taboo rather than intra-family
marriages. Lazer, in his population model, attempts to link
political stability to mortality and fertility rates.[17]

Sociologists have also conducted simulations of social influence models. Hanson and associates simulate the behavior or rural
migrants who have moved to an urban environment. McPhee simulates
the impact of interpersonal influence, personal predispositions,
and external persuasion of such migrants on their voting patterns.
Smith has used the same format of the McPhee model (i.e. stimula-
tion-discussion-learning) in his simulation of the effects of
leadership climates on army recruits' tendencies toward disobedi-
ence. Coleman has simulated the impact of friendship networks on
the smoking habits of high school students.[18]

The processing of social communications by individuals has
been studied through simulation. Abelson and Bernstein simulate
the diffusion of competing assertions in a community referendum
controversy, using a two-step model. In the first step, individual opinion change is affected by exposure to general mass communications media and special information channels. In the second
step, this change is reinforced through personal contact with
others.[19]

Pool and Kessler develop Crisiscom--a computer simulation of
national decision-makers processing information in a crisis. Each
message between actors has two components: affect or feeling
which the one actor has towad the other, and salience or importance of the other actor or interpersonal relationship to the
first actor. The model has three steps. Each actor receives
information about the world; each handles this information in ways
determined by his own background and by the model assumptions;

31

each then reacts by originating new messages. Pool and Kessler test this model with communications between the Tsar and the Kaiser from July 25, 1914 to July 31, 1914. Presumably the model put the most important of the numerous messages generated in an attention space. These authors claim the results verify their model.[20]

Gullahorn and Gullahorn develop a model of social exchange considerations in decision-making called Homunculus. They base their model on Homans' theory of elementary social behavior which sees an individual's responses as a function of the quantity and quality of reward and punishment his or her actions elicit. Using this model, Gullahorn and Gullahorn test hypotheses about role conflict resolution. Validating their model with interview data from union stewards, these authors claim a high correlation between the simulated and actual data sets.[21]

Pool, Abelson, and Poplin develop an electoral model for the 1964 election. They make three assumptions: all Democrats except those strongly opposed to civil rights would vote for Johnson; all Republicans would vote for Goldwater except those who supported the Democratic side on at least two out of three issue cluster; and all independents who expressed a clear view on civil rights would vote accordingly while those without a clear view on civil rights would vote with their other views. While these authors may be criticized for assuming no interpersonal contact, they found a .63 correlation between simulated and actual outcome.[22]

Legislative decision-making has served as a focus for political science modellers. Noting that the fate of most legislation is determined in committee rather than on the floor, Francis simulates committee decision-making in state legislatures. Using interview data from the Indiana State Assembly to develop his model, Francis employs factor analysis to simplify cognitive net structures through a reduction in variables. He then uses the emerging seven factors in the development of a model of committee decision-making called BPNS, or Binary Path Net Structuring.[23]

Shapiro simulates interactions pertaining to roll-call voting in the U.S. House of Representatives on the federal role in federal-state relations. He considers two processes: a cognitive process involving a representative's predisposition toward voting on a bill and a communication phase. In testing simulation output against votes in the Eighty-eighth Congress, the outcomes of all votes were correctly predicted, although the simulated splits in votes were larger than the actual votes.[24]

Pryor, an economist, uses computer simulation as a method of presenting a formal theory and examining the logical consequences

of that theory. He develops a most interesting model to explore
the influences of such a socioeconomic variables as patterns of
intergenerational grants, the rules of inheritance, differential
fertility of various income classes, and patterns of government
redistributions of income and wealth on overall income and wealth.
Pryor does not validate his model on the current size distribution
of income and wealth, arguing that the numerous simplifying assumptions make that impossible. Nevertheless, he contends that the
results of the model suggest that certain factors--in particular,
the shape of the inter-generational savings function--which have
previously been neglected by theorists are important in determining
size distribution of income and wealth.[25]

Like Francis, Manser, Naylor, and Wetz use a real data base
to develop a model which is then used to predict system outcome.
These authors develop an econometric model of state expenditures
on education. They then conduct computer simulation experiments
with the model to determine the effects of alternative federal
policies for allocating education funds to the states. Noting
that economic policy makers are typically interested not only in
whether alternatives differ, but also in how they differ, Manse,
Naylor, and Wetz examine six plans in terms of the state-federal
expenditure ratio and the distribution of income among the
states.[26]

Social scientists can develop computer simulation models for
the explicit purpose of aiding policy-makers in decision-making.
An example of a simulation created for this purpose is presented
by McEachern. Citing previous studies indicating that probation
programs have little effect on gang delinquency, McEachern
describes a simulation called Simbad developed to examine the
effectiveness of probation. Simbad uses Bayes decision rules of
conditional probability to place individuals in behavior categories. Simbad was tested against the actual data of delinquents
from seven counties in California. The simulation attempted to
predict whether juvenile behavior would get worse, stay the same,
or get better. Since Simbad predictions were moderately more
accurate than educated guessing, McEachern suggests that these
predictions could be used by probation officers to decide whether
to file a petition which is the equivalent of taking a juvenile
offender to court, to dismiss him, to refer him to another agency,
to put him on informal probation, or to continue formal
probation.[27]

Another example of a computer simulation model developed by
social scientists to facilitate policy making by decision-makers
is Manplan. Focusing on microbehavior within the jurisdiction of
a single supervisor in an organization, Miller and Haire developed
Manplan to serve as a tool of Management in manpower planning.
Manplan is not specific with respect to type of organization (i.e.

33

Manufacturing, sales, research, development, etc.), size of organization, formal structure of organization, and the identity and characteristics of incumbent individuals within the organization. Manplan included field-tested assumptions about the way supervisors evaluate their subordinates. The program can be run without random errors, or with any of four types of random errors: errors in supervisors' appraisal of subordinates, errors in the reward-giving process, errors in diagnosis, and errors in allocation. Current efforts are underway to validate the model at the G.E. Company.[28]

A simulation mentioned earlier of decision-making within organizations is the Garbage Can Model developed by Cohen, March, and Olsen. These authors incorporate three properties into their model which exemplify the organized anarchies they consider typical of organizational decision situations. The three properties are ill-defined preferences, unclear technology, and fluid participation. Four basic variables in the model are a stream of choices, a stream of problems, a rate of flow of solutions, and a stream of energy from participants. Two basic mapping processes are assumed: the mapping of choices onto decision makers, and the mapping of problems onto choices. Simplifying assumptions include an allocation of the energy of each participant to do more than one choice during each time period, attaching each problem to no more than one choice during each time period, and making energy requirements for a choice additive. Fixed parameters within the model include the number of time periods, the number of choice opportunities, the number of decision-makers, the number of problems, and the solution coefficients for the twenty time periods. Having created more realistic assumptions than previous organizational decision modellers, these authors then examine the effects of different decision structures on the decision process. These authors conclude by using the garbage can model to predict change within a university setting.[29]

What can we say about this random sampling of computer simulation models in the social sciences? Several things come to mind. First, it seems that social scientists can simulate and have simulated an extremely diverse array of systems, ranging from internal psychological processes occuring within a single human being to large, complex, and interactive social, organizational, political, and economic systems. This appears to be a distinct advantage of computer simulation modelling over alternative modes of analysis. As we stated earlier, any system which can be specified by symbolic terms and logical processes can be simulated. By contrast, the universe of applications for mathematical and statistical analysis is somewhat more restricted. While verbal analysis may be applied to any type of problem, it may not be as inherently illuminating as simulation on the digital computer; verbal analysis also lacks many of the other

34

organizational variables such as degree of hierarchy and span of control upon the individual decision process when the individual is faced with choosing between innovation and lack of innovation. Ultimately we hope to logically confirm hypotheses concerning the relationship between internal organizational control variables and organizational decisions to pursue policy innovation. First, however, let us look more closely at the nature of simulation and modelling, so that we understand the strengths and limitations of the methodological technique we employ.

Footnotes, Chapter Two:

[1] Chris Argyris, "Some Limits of Rational Man Organizational Theory," Public Administration Review, Vol. 33, No. 3, (May-June 1973), pp. 253-267.

[2] Charles E. Lindblom, "The Science of Muddling Through," Public Administration Review, Vol. 29, (Spring 1959), pp. 1-86.

[3] Argyris.

[4] Paul Samuelson, Economics: An Introductory Analysis (New York: McGraw-Hill, Inc., 1967), pp. 474-482.

[5] Grant McConnell, Private Power and American Democracy (New York: Alfred A. Knopf, 1966), pp. 11-29.

[6] R. E. Marsten, W. W. Hogan, and J. W. Blankenship, "The Boxstep Method for Large-Scale Optimization," Operations Research, Vol. 23, No. 3 (May-June, 1975), pp. 389-405.

[7] Numerous articles in the business literature illustrate this point including the following:

W. D. Cook, M. J. L. Kirby, and S. L. Mehndiretta, "A Linear Fractional Max-Min Problem," Operations Research, Vol. 23, No. 3 (May-June 1975), pp. 511-512. This article deals with a generalized case of the fractionalized max-min problem prevalent in the literature which is equivalent to a quasi-convex programming problem whose optimal solution lies at the vortex of the feasible region.

Graham McMahon and Michael Florian, "On Scheduling with Ready Times and Due Dates to Minimize Maximum Lateness," Operations Research, Vol. 23, No. 3 (May-June 1975), pp. 475-482. These authors develop a brancy-and-bound method to sequence jobs on a single processor in order to minimize maximum lateness, subject to ready times and due dates. An unusual feature of this method

as well as a function of his or her ability to engage in such search activities. Motivation to search out innovative alternatives is directly related to the individual's dissatisfaction with the status quo; the ability to search for innovative alternatives is directly related to the resources an individual has at his or her disposal which have been allocated for this purpose, or which at least have not been allocated for another purpose.

The third new assumption is to recognize that, <u>ceteris paribus</u>, sunk or fixed costs bias the decision-maker toward the status quo. This assumption of sunk costs is widely recognized by both economists and accountants, as well as politicians who are unwilling to choose innovative alternatives in the middle of a war or to discontinue the development of a sophisticated expensive weapons system because of previously sunk investment. Here we shall refer to sunk or fixed costs to mean expenditures for assets which can be used only if the status quo is perpetuated and which must be discarded or lost if an innovative alternative is selected.

The fourth new assumption of our model of innovative decision-making is to acknowledge that the payoff from any innovative alternative is not absolutely certain prior to engaging in the alternative, but rather contains a certain element of risk. That any innovative alternative contains a certain amount of risk, and that the risk may vary from a great deal to very little is widely accepted by business managers, public administrators, financial consultants, and political advisors. Two techniques employed to minimize risks associated with innovative alternatives are the development of contingency plans and diversification of assets.

The fifth new assumption is that individuals vary as to their willingness to take risks. This assumption that individuals have varying degrees of willingness to take risks has been empirically verified by David McClelland in his work on entrepreneurship and need achievement.[19] McClelland found that entrepreneurs had greater willingness to take moderate risks than did persons pursuing other occupations, and that approximately fifty years after a large number of these persons appeared in a country, a considerable spurt of economic growth and development occurred.

Armed with these additional assumptions which have expanded our traditional rational choice model into one which more accurately reflects the process whereby an individual decides to pursue policy innovation or to reject it in favor of perpetuating the status quo, we shall establish a more detailed algorithm depicting this individual decision-making process. Then we shall look at how the decisions of individuals are passed through a hierarchical organization, at how individual decisions become translated into organizational decisions, and at the effect of

23

on decision-making within bureaucratic organizations. Specifically, we shall generate hypotheses concerning two major dependent variables: one is the total number of organizational decisions made where the status quo is rejected in favor of an innovative alternative; the second is the rate of cumulative innovation change over a specified time period. We shall distinguish between an individual decision and an organizational decision. The model presupposes that every individual in the organization is capable of making decisions between perpetuating the status quo and choosing an innovative alternative which may be passed upward to his or her superior, and in fact does so. However, only certain individuals have the authority to make organizational decisions--that is, decisions in which the organization commits resources in hopes of securing some gain. The number of authoritative individuals who can make organizational decisions is one of the organizational variables to be tested in the model.

Our innovation model modifies the traditional rational choice model within an organizational context to achieve greater conformity with reality. From the rational choice model we adopt the assumptions of satisfaction maximization which is approximated by resource maximization, as well as benefit-cost analysis to determine priorities among policy alternatives. Recognizing that resources are the best easily measured surrogate of satisfaction, economists have adopted this technique of equating utility maximization with income maximization for both individuals and organizations.[17] Downs also argues that bureaus have an inherent tendency to expand; since organizations cannot expand without resources, they seek to maximize resource units at their disposal.[18] Unlike the traditional rational choice model, we shall make five additional assumptions both to take into account criticisms of the traditional model and to make our basic model assumptions more realistic.

The first new assumption of our innovative decision-making model or expanded rational choice model is to recognize the limitations of human intellect by limiting the number of alternatives potentially available to an individual in any given decision situation. We assume that the number of alternatives potentially available to any individual in any decision situation is not unlimited, but rather is limited by both the individual's inherent intellectual capacity to grasp and deal with different alternatives at any point in time and by the degree to which innovative alternatives to the status quo have been discovered and promulgated in any given policy area.

The second new assumption is derived from March and Simon; we assume that the number of alternatives available to an individual in any given decision situation is not a given, but is a function of the motivation of the individual to search them out,

22

most theories of choice have not distinguished between the alternative of continuing and alternatives of change, these authors
contend that an adequate theory of innovation would not treat the
two symmetrically. The alternative of continuing must be differ-
entiated from alternatives of change by coupling the latter with
a theory of search for new alternatives.[15] Hence, the main argument of Simon and March is that innovative alternatives should be
treated differently from the status quo in a rational choice
model. From these hypotheses of these authors, we shall incorporate sunk costs, innovation or search costs, and dissatisfaction
with the status quo as a motivation to search out alternatives to
the status quo into our innovative decision-making model.

An additional concept incorporated into our decision-making
model is that of non-decisions. Non-decisions have long been
recognized by political scientists as having an impact on policy
outcomes.[16] In effect, a non-decision is a decision to do nothing,
or in this case, a decision to avoid innovative actions and to
perpetuate the status quo. The concept of non-decisions implicitly
recognizes the significance of time in a decision-making model.
In any given time period, decisions and non-decisions occur--that
is, decisions to innovate and decisions to perpetuate the status
quo take place. To simplify matters, our model here will establish
a one-to-one equivalency between time periods and decision-making
periods. In twenty time periods, for example, an individual can
make and does make twenty decisions. Each of the twenty may be
a "real" decison in that the individual chooses to pursue an
innovative alternative, or it may be a "non-decision" in that he
chooses to do nothing and to therefore perpetuate the status quo.

Bachrach and Baratz delineate four types of non-decison-
making: invocation of force to prevent demands for change; use
of power to make threats of sanctions against initiators of
potentially threatening demands; invocation of an existing bias
in the political system such as a norm, precedent, rule, or procedure to prevent a demand for change; and reshaping or strenghen-
ing the mobilization of bias to block change demands. A fifth
situation similar to non-decision-making will more closely
resemble that of our model, for the rules or procedures of chain
of command and hierarchial flow of decisions may be invoked by a
risk-averting superior to ignore the demands or suggestions of
his subordinates for innovation.

The Innovation Simulation Model:

The primary concepts underlying this innovation model are not
original to this author. The originality of this book lies in the
author's development of a dynamic probabilistic simulation model,
and the utilization of this to logically confirm or fail to confirm hypotheses concerning the impact of organizational variables

advantages of computer simulation modelling which we shall discuss. While other modes of analysis may sometimes force the researcher to think in a holistic manner, computer model simulation emphasizes the functional relationship between the various parts or components of the system and the system as a whole.[30]

A second point which strikes us when recalling the sampling of computer simulation models developed by social scientists is the diversity of forms of simulation. Simulations may present a formal theory only, or present a formal account of empirical data, or use some combination of the two. The simulations developed by Pryor; Cohen, March, and Olsen and at this point, Miller and Haire fit into the first category of presenting a formal theory. Francis, on the one hand, and Manser, Naylor, and Wetz on the other hand use empirical data presented in a formal account as a basis for building a simulation model. Francis employs factor analysis on empirical data to develop factors simplifying the cognitive structure of relevant simulation actors. Manser, Naylor, and Wetz develop an econometric model of state expenditures on education, using empirical data. These two types of simulation are combined in the works of Pool and Kessler; Gullahorn and Gullahorn; Shapiro; Pool, Ableson, and Poplin; and McEachern. The fact that there are multiple ways simulations can be developed and conducted signifies the flexibility of this method as a tool of analysis.

A third point which strikes us about the social science simulations we reviewed is the large number of variables frequently included within the framework of any one model. The simulation presented by Pryor had numerous independent variables pertaining to the fertility rates of different income groups, the division of wealth between children, the marriageability of individuals, government redistributive actions, etc. Simbad, which dealt with juvenile offenders had twenty independent simulation variables. Similarly, to a greater or lesser extent, most of the other simulations discussed had numerous variables. This ability of the researcher to include numerous variables in a computer simulation model in specific and precise terms facilitates unambiguous formulation of theory as well as the inclusion of sufficient detail so as not to severely distort reality. This unambiguous theory formulation and detail inclusion may be seen as an advantage of computer model simulation.

Fourthly, in all the models, input variables did not become transformed directly into output, but rather first went through one or more simulation processes. Thus, computer simulation allows the researcher to manipulate the major components of a complex system in laboratory situations without actually constructing or physically replicating the system itself. In this way, the cost, inconvenience, and time involved in experimentation on the actual system itself or on small scale versions of it can be avoided. Due to political considerations or the irreversible nature of the change process in the real world, such experimentation in many cases is not only costly, but also impossible, leaving the use of computer models as the only practical means of obtaining accurate information on which to plan and design new systems.[31] The works of Pool and Kessler, Francis, and Shapiro are just a few examples of this point. Reitman applauds the value of computer models under these conditions. According to Reitman, the development of a model and the use of simulation are invaluable tools of the system designer: while the system is still a paper concept he or she can operate the system and manipulate major components without regard for real world restraints, limited funds, and tight schedules.[32]

Hence, a computer model simulation sets up a laboratory situation frequently lacking in social science by allowing the variation of variables one at a time, holding other variables constant. Not only can the researcher determine the relative impacts of different variables, but her or she can also determine at what stages of the processes relative impact occur. Because the logical processes and assumptions in a simulation model may reasonably reflect reality, but the variance of input variables fed into the model may not exist in the real world, some would contend that the model merely becomes an exercise in logical deduction. This characteristic of computer simulation models, however, may be viewed as a strength as well as a weakness. By varying input variables beyond their current state in reality, extreme conditions which would cause the model to "blow up" may be determined. Such information could be very useful to social planners and cannot be obtained from other types of analysis. Similarly, if the real world system is static and change is desired, computer simulation allows assessment of the minimum change in system input variables necessary to achieve the desired change in system output. The Manser, Naylor, and Wetz simulation provides an illustration of the utilization of computer models for the purpose of examining the effect of input variables with a range exceeding their real world variation on output. We may recall that these authors examine the effects of six alternative federal policies for allocating educational funds to the states, only one of which could possibly be in existence.

A fifth feature of the simulations created by social scientists is of interest. All the computer simulation models we reviewed here were dynamic in nature; they included time as an independent variable. Schechter notes that "Characteristically, the output of a dynamic model is in the form of time series of the endogenous variables."[33] Two advantages may be attributed to

36

dynamic models, as opposed to static models. Dynamic models can be said to be more reflective of reality, since time does impact to a greater or lesser extent on real world systems. Also, most static models tend to be equilibrium models. We could argue that equilibrium models do not adequately describe, explain, and predict numerous social phenomena, for many real world systems do not, in actuality, strive toward equilibrium. Interactive social exchanges may fall in this category, an illustration being the work of Pool and Kessler. Two potential problems created by dynamism are auto-correlation among observations of a given series and biased simulation output caused by the impact of initial conditions on system behavior.[34]

A sixth feature of the social science simulations reviewed here is the occasional inclusion of stochastic disturbances within the model. Miller and Haire, for example, included the option of introducing different types of random errors in their Manplan program. Using a random number generation technique to either distribute input variables or to determine the outcome of decision rules also introduces stochastic variation in simulation results. This, in effect, causes a simulation run to become one of many in a probability distribution. Variability in the endogenous variables--i.e. the output data--is introduced by the inclusion of stochastic elements in the simulation model, causing the numerical results of a single run to become a sample of one from some empirical probability distribution.[35]

Introducing output variance through the inclusion of stochastic elements has both advantages and disadvantages. A disadvantage of the inclusion of stochastic variation in computer simulation models is that the researcher cannot always produce the exact same results with replication. He or she must use a number of replications and talk about results in terms of statistical probabilities rather than as stated facts. An advantage of the inclusion of stochastic variation in computer simulation models is that such variation more closely resembles the random forces present in the real world.[36]

Until now we have mainly discussed beneficial or positive aspects of computer model simultations. However, from our review of a sample of models developed by social scientists, we realize that not all is wine and roses. In the process of simulating, the modeller may lose sight of the goal of understanding the system being modelled by becoming distracted by such computer problems as how to overcome storage limitations or whether the program is sufficiently elegant. Finding programming errors, while very necessary, may be particularly time and interest consuming. Finding all programming errors is essential, but may become a distraction from the primary simulation goal of building a reasonable model and examining its implications under varying conditions. The fact that one programming error is sufficient to invalidate the whole model is an advantage in ensuring precision, but it simultaneously serves as a disadvantage in frustration and wasting time in the debugging process. Because computers do not yet have the technical capacity to be programmed for pattern recognition, the computer has only limited ability to electroni-check for programming errors in a simulation model. Substantial time and effort must still be exerted by the researcher to check for model and input accuracy.[37]

While we have contended that computer simulation models could be developed for any system whose components can be expressed in precise symbols and logical processes, there is a certain minimum complexity of interrelated ideas that is probably necessary to make a theoretical scheme worth putting in the form of a computer program. Most of the models we reviewed were sophisticated and complex. A theoretical idea so simple that its implications in the form of a model are predictable and obvious is not advantageous to program. Hence, theoretical simplicity may serve as a real limitation to the use of computer model simulation.[38]

Frequently, with computer simulation models, the researcher experiences difficulty translating information about the model to the reader. This problem is compounded when the reader is inexperienced with the technique of simulation. While a set of ideas may be demonstrated vividly through an adequately documented computer program, describing the detailed program which exemplifies these ideas may be difficult. It is usually not possible within the space of a research paper to provide a complete description, and even if it were possible, the reader could easily become lost in the wealth of detail.[39] Apter concludes that the best solution to this problem may be to describe the program by means of flow diagrams which give an idea of the logical structure of the program, and to make clear what are the theoretical idea underlying the program. Frijda also comments on this communication problem. He notes that nothing in a computer program distinguishes embodied theory from programming techniques and short cuts. When the researcher verbally explains the program, delineating theory from technique for the reader, much of the clarity and precision of the computer model is lost in the translation.[40]

Finding a solution to the communication problem is not a simple matter. The benefits of computer simulation are negated by global informal descriptions yet frequently publishing the programs seems neither feasible nor useful. Frijda contends that the best road lies between these two extremes. He feels it will in general be possible to describe the relevant processes unambiguously by naming the subroutines concerned, and by stating their precise input and output condition, the conditions of their activation, and the transformations they achieve. Also, it will generally be possible to do this completely in the sense of mentioning all tests, parameters, etc. upon which these outputs depend without leaving the level of theoretically relevant subroutines and without descending into technical detail. For this approach to work, two requirements must be met: the program structure must reflect the structure of the theory, and the statement of the theoretically important program segments should contain all details without auxiliary operations and other conditions (e.g. memory storage registers, counters) which influence or co-determine the operation of main routines.[41]

A major problem with computer simulation models is the difficulty of evaluating program performance. Frequently computer models present a formal theory with no empirical validation of the simulation output. Almost invariably, when empirical validation is provided, it consists of one case or situation where simulated results moderately resemble real world occurrences. Almost never do simulation modellers provide evidence of more than one situation where the model correctly predicts real world events. In these instances, the modeller has validated his or her creation only to the extent that a case study validates a complex social theory. From our review of social science simulations, we may recall that Shapiro validated his model with selected roll calls from the 88th Congress. Why the 88th, rather than the 80th, 85th, 87th, or the 80th through the 88th Congress, we might ask? Is his model good for predictions in most Congresses, or only for selected roll call votes in the 88th Congress? We don't know. Pool and Kessler validated their model of interaction between political elite interactions with data from interactions between the Tsar and Kaiser. Does their model also apply to interactions between Kruschev and Kennedy during the Cuban Missle Crisis? How about to current interactions between Jewish and Arab leaders? Or to messages between Indian and Pakistani leaders during the Bangledesh crisis? How about to messages between political elites in non-crisis situations? Again we don't know. These two studies are not particularly unique in their single situation validation of models, for reasons we shall discuss. One isolated simulation in the literature attempting multiple instances of validation was developed by Crecine. Crecine develops a computer simulation model of municipal budgeting which he validates with empirical data from the 1956-1965 Cleveland budgets, the 1958-1965 Detroit budgets, and the 1960-1965 Pittsburgh budgets. While Crecine used only northern cities in or on the fringe of the Great Lakes industrial belt, he may nonetheless be commended for his attempts at multiple validation.[42]

Frijda divides the evaluation of program performance into two separate and distinct activities: the first activity is

39

evaluation of the program's contributions to the academic discipline in question--that is the evaluation of the value of the theory; the second activity is the evaluation of the fit between program output and behavior--or predictive accuracy.[43] The first activity is the primary mode of evaluating simulations whose sole purpose is to present a formal theory and to examine the logical implications of that theory in a dynamic environment. Such a model was presented by Pryor in his study of factors impacting of the size distribution of income and wealth. By incorporating social and cultural variables usually excluded from econometric models, Pryor was able to show the significance of factors impacting on the size distribution of income and wealth which had previously been ignored by economists.

The second evaluation activity focuses on predictive accuracy. Almost no methodology had been developed for measuring the fit between the program output and behavior. While much ingenuity has been devoted to the development of programs, little attention has been given to the assessment of their value. Hence, high precision is juxtaposed with spots of rough approximations which [44] undercut the very precision of higher language computer programs. Scheter perceptively comments on aspects of the problem of empirical validation of computer model simulation, and notes that validation is a more acute problem in simulation than in other models which are solved analytically.

There are three reasons empirical validation of simulation models and findings is difficult. First, many simulation models are quite large, employing a great number of functional relationships, each of which is based on one or more behavioral assumptions. Secondly, simulation models usually include a large number of output variables, frequently appearing in the form of time series. Both of these points indicate an incredibly large set of real world data would be necessary to validate functional relationships, behavioral assumptions, and time series output variables. A third difficulty results from a lack of universal agreement as to which of the multitude of validation strategies and approaches is most appropriate in any particular situation.[45] A researcher may claim validation for a model if simulated and real world input conditions match on the one hand, and simulated and real world output conditions are reasonable approximations on the other hand, without empirically validating simulated intermediate steps, processes, and decision criteria. Hence, a "validated" computer simulation model may incorporate unrealistic intermediate steps, processes and decision criteria. Consequently, when environmental conditions not represented or misrepresented in the model change in the real world, the computer simulation model may no longer provide reasonably accurate predictions.

40

Briefly, let us consider why the technique of computer simulation is suitable to our analysis of innovative decision-making in organizations. The bureaucratic organization is a complex system. Inputs in the form of demands placed upon the organization, and resources and choices available to it; conversion processes in the form of survival mechanisms developed; and outputs in the form of policies, products, and programs are all part of the organizational system. Also, any organization experiences both positive feedback which reinforces previously chosen policies and negative feedback which eventually foments a search for new alternatives. As a complex system where human decisions play a primary role in determining organizational output, the bureaucratic organization has not in the past lent itself readily to mathematical formulations, although there are no intrinsic problems with such an approach. Traditionally, analyses of bureaucratic decision-making have relied upon a verbal description of demands, information, and decision flows on a case by case basis. Harold Stein's classic textbook Public Administration and Policy Development represents this approach.[46] In addition to a lack of precision, generalizations from the findings of one case to other bureaucratic organizations may be difficult; frequently, explanatory theory is lacking. By contrast, computer simulation allows us to make specific realistic assumptions about organizations and to build a dynamic model using clearly defined relations and decision criteria. With this model we can copy organizational phenomena in programming language as well as control for extraneous events and phenomena, thereby deriving many of the benefits of a laboratory situation without many of the costs.

Footnotes, Chapter Three:

[1] Frederick L. Whitney, The Elements of Research (New York: Prentice-Hall, Inc., 1950), pp. 1-10.

[2] Alpha C. Chiang, Fundamental Methods of Mathematical Economics (New York: McGraw-Hill, Inc., 1967), pp. 8-11.

[3] John Smith, Computer Simulation Models (New York: Hafner Publishing Co., 1968), p. 3

[4] George S. Fishman, Concepts and Methods in Discrete Event Digital Simulation (John Wiley and Sons, Inc., 1973), p. 4.

[5] Smith, p. 4.

[6] Mordechai Schechter, "On the Use of Computer Simulation for Research," Simulation and Games, Vol. 2, No. 1 (March 1971), p. 73.

[7] Fishman, p. 4.

[8] Ibid., pp. 7-8.

[9] Smith, p. 3.

[10] Herbert Maisel and Giuliano Gnuglino, Simulation of Discrete Stochastic Systems (Science Research Association, Inc., 1972), p. 4.

[11] Julian Reitman, Computer Simulation Applications (New York: John Wiley and Sons, Inc., 1971), p. 7.

[12] Smith, p. 3.

[13] Reitman, p. 7.

[14] Fishman, p. 11.

[15] Ibid., pp. 6-7.

[16] Ibid., p. 1.

[17] Jeane E. and John T. Gullahorn "Simulation and Social Science Theory: The State of the Union," Simulation and Games, Vol. 1, No. 1 (March 1970), pp. 21-26.

[18] Ibid., pp. 28-31.

[19] Ibid., p. 32.

[20] Ithiel de Sola Pool and Allan Kessler, "The Kaiser, the Tsar, and the Computer: Information Processing in a Crisis," American Behaviorial Scientists, Vol. 8, No. 8 (April 1968), pp. 31-38.

[21] John T. Gullahorn and Jeanne E. Gullahorn, "Some Computer Applications in Social Sciences," American Sociological Review, Vol. 30, No. 3 (June 1965), pp. 355-358.

[22] Ithiel de Sola Pool, Robert P. Abelson, and Sammuel L. Poplin, "A Postscript on the 1964 Election," American Behavioral Scientist, Vol. 8, No. 8 (April 1965), pp. 39-44.

[23] Wayne L. Francis, "Simulation of Committee Decision-Making in a State Legislative Body," Simulation and Games, Vol. 1, No. 3 (September 1970), pp. 235-262.

[24] Michael J. Shapiro, "The House and the Federal Role: A Computer Simulation of Roll-Call Voting," American Political Science Review, Vol. 62, No. 2 (June 1968).

[25] Frederic L. Pryor, "Simulation of the Impact of Social and Economic Institutions on the Size Distribution of Income and Wealth," American Economic Review, Vol. 63, No. 1 (March 1973), pp. 50-72.

[26] Marilyn E. Manser, Thomas H. Naylor, and Kenneth L. Wetz, "Effects of Alternative Policies for Allocating Federal Aid for Education to the States," Simulation and Games, Vol. 1, No. 2 (June 1970), pp. 135-154.

[27] A. W. McEachern, ed., "The Juvenile Probation Simulation: Simulation for Research and Decision-Making," American Behavioral Scientist, Vol. 11, No. 3 (Jan-Feb., 1968), pp. 1-48.

[28] James R. Miller, III, and Mason Haire, "Manplan: A Micro-Simulator for Manpower Planning," Behavioral Science, Vol. 15 (November 1970), pp. 524-531.

[29] Michael D. Cohen, James G. March, and Johan P. Olsen, "A Garbage Can Model of Organizational Choice," Administrative Science Quarterly, Vol. 17 (March 1972), pp. 1-25.

[30] Michael J. Apter, The Computer Simulation of Behavior (London: Hutchinson & Co., Ltd., 1970), p. 26.

[31] Smith, p. 4.

[32] Reitman, p. 7.

[33] Schechter, p. 84.

[34] Ibid., p. 85.

[35] Ibid., p. 83.

[36] Ibid., p. 83.

[37] Apter, p. 27.

[38] Ibid., p. 27.

[39] Ibid., p. 27.

[40] Nico H. Frijda, "Problems of Computer Simulation," Computer Simulation of Human Behavior, eds. John M. Dutton and William H. Starbuck (New York: John Wiley & Sons, Inc., 1971), p. 611.

[41] Ibid., p. 611.

[42] Ibid., p. 611.

[43]Frijda, p. 613.

[44]Ibid., p. 613.

[45]Schechter, p. 86.

[46]Harold Stein, Public Administration and Policy Development, (New York: Harcourt, Brace, and World, Inc., 1952), pp. 860.

CHAPTER FOUR

Methodology and Model Development

In order to test hypotheses about the numbers of innovations
produced by different types of organizations, we will develop and
use a dynamic probabilistic simulation model. The purpose of
this analysis is to present a formal theory of innovative
decision-making in organizations and to examine the logical consequences of that theory under varying organizational structures.
Specifically, we shall examine hypotheses concerning two major
dependent variables: one is the total number of organizational
decisions made where the status quo is rejected in favor of an
innovative alternative; the second is the rate of innovation in
the organization over a specified time period.

In the innovation model, we distinguish between an individual
decision and an organizational decision. The model presupposes
that every individual in the organization is capable of making and
in fact, every time period does make decisions between perpetuating the status quo and choosing an innovative alternative which
may be passed upward to his or her superior. However, only certain individuals have the authority to make organizational
decisions--that is, decisions in which the organization commits
resources in hopes of securing some gain. The number of authoritative individuals who can make organizational decisions is one of
the organizational variables to be tested in the model.

There are two basic algorithms which are used in each time
period. The first algorithm represents the process whereby the
individual makes two basic decisions: the first decision is
whether or not the individual will engage in search activities to
discover alternatives to the status quo; the second decision is
whether or not the individual will choose to recommend to his or
her superior that the status quo be rejected in favor of an innovative alternative he or she has discovered in the search
activities. We shall call this first algorithm the individual
processing algorithm. The second algorithm locates authoritative
individuals within the organization and determines two things
also: the first is whether or not the authoritative individual
will attempt to commit resources to an innovative alternative;
the second is whether or not the authoritative individual's
attempts to enact an innovation are successful. We shall call
this second algorithm the organizational processing algorithm.

We shall examine each algorithm in more detail. Part one of
the individual processing algorithm focuses on the individual's
decision to engage in search activities for innovative alternatives. This part of the first algorithm assumes that information

is not a free commodity. Information is a resource of one type, and in order to acquire it, an individual must give up resources of another type. In the model, an individual can engage in search activities only if he or she has a positive amount of resource units. This part of the individual processing algorithm also assumes that an individual does not engage in search activities randomly but does so only if he or she is dissatisfied with the status quo. In the model, the amount of search activity on the part of an individual for innovative alternatives is directly and positively related to the amount of resources he or she holds which are specifically available for search activities. Organizational slack is a concept used here to denote organizational resources not committed to ongoing programs, but which are potentially free to be used for non-organizational goal-directed purposes. If either an individual's resources exceeds his or her dissatisfaction, or his or her dissatisfaction exceeds his or her resources, then the lesser of the two factors becomes the limit placed on the individual's search activities for that time period.

To determine, once an individual has engaged in search activities, whether to recommend to his superior to perpetuate the status quo or to engage in an innovative alternative, the individual undergoes the process in part two of the individual processing algorithm. Essentially, he or she conducts a risk check, a resource check, and a benefit-cost analysis weighted toward the status quo. This risk check consists of determining whether the individual's risk factor is at least as great as the risk factor of the choice. Individuals are assumed to have varying degrees of willingness to take calculated risks, a phenomena represented in this model by the attachment of risk factors or numbers indicating willingness to take calculated risks to individuals. Risk factors are also attached to choices, indicating the degree of risk involved in the organization realizing the choice payoff. In the risk check, individuals only accept choices which have risks equal to or less than their own risk factors. The resource check consists of determining whether the total organizational resources are at least as great as the total cost of the choice; if not, the innovative alternative is rejected. Individuals in public agencies usually have information available as to amounts of total organizational resources, for total bureau resources are specified annually (or every two years in some states) in advance in the budget process. The weighted benefit-cost ratio is conducted for all innovative choices passing the first two checks and for the status quo. The benefit-cost ratio for an innovative choice is equal to the choice payoff divided by the total costs of the choice. The status quo benefit-cost ratio is equal to the status quo payoff divided by the quantity, total costs of the status quo minus sunk costs of the status quo. The individual then chooses the alternative--whether it is innovative or status quo--with the highest benefit-cost ratio. The benefit-cost ratio is weighted toward the status quo under the assumption that part of the initial outlay for any alternative is for fixed assets and start-up costs, and consequently represents an expenditure of resources that does not have to be replicated in each time period subsequent to the initial one.

One definition of degree of hierarchy in this innovation model simulation is the probability that a superior will consult his or her subordinates in any given decision situation. Individuals conducting the benefit-cost calculus who have subordinates have a certain probability of including recommendations from their subordinates in their analysis. If an individual does consider the recommendation of one of his or her subordinates, he or she does so without any additional expenditure of resources on his or her part, for the subordinate's recommendation is made available not through any resources spending search activities on his or her own, but rather through the authority of his or her position as superior in an organizational hierarchy.

Let us now look at the organizational processing algorithm. The first part, which locates authoritative individuals capable of committing organizational resources, is simple. Essentially, any individual in the organization situated above a given level has such authority. Authoritative individuals with superiors can make recommendations to those superiors which may or may not be accepted; however, those authoritative individuals can commit organizational resources in decision-making in their own right. Essentially any individual in the organization situated above a given level has such authority. The level in the organization to which a recommendation must pass before it is considered to be an organizational decision is a definition of decentralization used in this innovation model simulation. All authoritative individuals are checked to see if they recommend alternatives differing from the status quo. For each authoritative individual who recommends an innovative alternative, a probability test of successful adoption of the innovation is conducted as a second part of the organizational processing algorithm. The probability test has a probability of success equal to the risk factor of the choice; its utilization assumes that factors exogenous to the model affect the outcome of an attempt by an organization to adopt an innovative alternative. If the probability test is positive, the innovative alternative is successfully adopted. If the probability test is negative, the status quo is perpetuated. Authoritative individuals are checked in a top to bottom, left to right procedure, according to the positions of the individuals in the organizational hierarchy. In terms of the order of decision-making of authoritative individuals, organizational hierarchy where preference is usually given to those higher up the hierarchy provides justification for the top to bottom bias. While the same rationale does not justify the left to right bias, values attached to individuals, including

authoritative individuals, were distributed randomly initially;
consequently, there is no reason to suspect that individuals
occupying positions on the left hand side of the organization
differ in any substantial way from individuals on the right hand
side, or that a left hand bias differs in any substantial way
from a right hand bias.

For illustrative purposes, let us consider a numerical
example of the individual and organizational processing algorithms.
Given an organization with a span of control of two, we shall
focus on two subordinates and their immediate superior. We shall
assume that the individual risk factor, the individual resources
units, and the dissatisfaction factor attached to the superior are
five, three, and seven, respectfully. In addition, we shall
assume that comparable values attached to subordinate one are two,
six, and eight, while nine, ten, and four are attached to subordinate two. Furthermore, we shall assume that the benefit-cost
ratio of the status quo is 1.10 and total organizational resources
are 840.

In part one of the individual processing algorithm, each
individual in the organization determines whether or not to engage
in search activities for innovative alternatives. We may recall
the model assumption which directly relates individual search
activity to the individual's resource units and level of dissatisfaction with the status quo, with the lesser of the two placing a
limit on search activity. Since the superior has three resource
units and a dissatisfaction level of seven, he or she will search
three choices for an innovative alternative more suitable than the
status quo. Subordinate one will search six choices, while subordinate two will search four. The case of subordinate two
illustrates the point that an extremely high value for either dissatisfaction or resources does not necessarily result in massive
search activities by the individual unless the high value for one
individual factor occurs simultaneously with a high value for the
other factor.

In the second part of the individual processing algorithm,
the individual searches through an appropriate number of choices
seeking a suitable alternative to the status quo. In each case,
choices are randomly selected from a stream of choices created in
the initial stages of the simulation. We may recall that each
choice has a risk factor, a payoff factor, a total cost factor,
and a fixed or sunk cost factor attached to it. In this stage of
the individual processing algorithm, the organizational member
conducts several checks. For the purposes of illustration, let
us focus on the superior who is motivated and able to search three
choices, and who has an individual risk factor of five. Let us
assume that the three choices randomly and sequentially selected
by the superior have the following values attached to their risk,

payoff, total cost, and sunk cost factors: Choice 21 (9, 500, 400, 80); Choice 4 (3, 200, 800, 160); Choice 17 (5, 600, 400, 80).

The organizational member, in his or her search, first conducts a risk check. In the case of Choice 21, the superior we are examining checks to see if the risk factor of the choice is less than or equal to his or her own risk factor. Since nine, the risk factor of the choice is not less than or equal to five, the individual risk factor of the superior, he or she abandons further investigatory activity related to this choice and goes on to the next randomly selected choice. Choice 4 passes the risk check since three, the risk factor of the choice, is less than five, the individual risk factor. The superior then conducts a resource check to determine if the total cost of the choice is less than or equal to the total resources of the organization. Since 800 is less than 840, Choice 4 meets this condition. The third check compares the benefit-cost ratio of the choice to the benefit-cost ratio of the status quo. Since the benefit-cost ratio of Choice 4 (200/800 = .25) is less than the benefit-cost ratio of the status quo (1.10), Choice 4 is likewise abandoned. The third randomly selected alternative, Choice 17, passes both the risk and resource checks. Because the benefit-cost ratio of Choice 17 (600/400 = 1.5) exceeds the benefit-cost ratio of the status quo (1.10), this particular superior decides to recommend that Choice 17 be adopted in lieu of the status quo in this time period.

The process of searching through an appropriate number of choices is repeated for subordinate one, subordinate two, and each and every other individual member of the organization. Here we shall assume that subordinate one, as a consequence of his or her search, recommends perpetuation of the status quo, while subordinate two recommends Choice 18 (4, 300, 100, 20). Further, we shall assume a .5 degree of hierarchy--that is, a probability of .5 that any superior will consult the recommendations of his or her subordinates. In part two of the individual processing algorithm, a probability test weighted by the hierarchical probability test results in our example are positive for subordinate one and negative for subordinate two. Our superior consults subordinate one, checking to see if the risk factor of the choice recommended by subordinate one is less than or equal to his or her risk factor, and if the benefit-cost ratio of the subordinate's recommendation is greater than that of his or her own recommendation. As subordinate one recommends the status quo (risk factor = 0), the risk check is passed, but the benefit-cost ratio check is not passed (1.10 is not greater than 1.5). Choice 18, the recommendation of subordinate two, is potentially more desirable to our superior than Choice 17, his or her actual recommendation, since the risk factor of Choice 18 (4) is less than five, the superior's individual risk factor, and the benefit-cost ratio of Choice 18 (300/100 = 3) is greater than that of Choice 17 (1.5). However, the hierarchical probability test for subordinate two was negative. As a result, the superior does not consult subordinate two. Our superior retains his or her original recommendation of Choice 17.

In the organizational processing algorithm, authoritative individuals capable of committing bureau resources are located. In the interest of simplicity, we shall assume that our superior is the only authoritative individual in the organization. Should the authoritative individual recommend an alternative different from the status quo, as is the case, a probability test weighted by (.1) times the risk factor of the choice being considered is conducted. In our example the probability weight would be .5. If the results should be positive, Choice 17 is adopted and becomes the status quo. Organizational resources increase by a factor determined by the benefit-cost ratio (1.5 times 840 = 1,260). The new benefit-cost ratio of the status quo becomes even more favorable as sunk costs are disregarded in subsequent calculations [600/(400 - 80) = 1.875]. If the results of the probability test should be negative, Choice 17 is not adopted and total organizational resources are diminished by choice total costs (840 - 400 = 440). Next, a replacement alternative for Choice 17 is generated, dissatisfaction levels of individual organizational members may be adjusted on the basis of their recommendations in the previous four time periods, and the two basic algorithms are reiterated in the next time period.

In the innovation model simulation, decisions represent choice between non-conflictual policy alternatives. Three assumptions are made about the nature of choices in this model. First, choices do not deal with internal personnel matters or organizational structure. Personnel matters are excluded from the scope of decision-making because there are no provisions within the innovation model in its current state to remove or add organizational members, or to shift individuals around from position to position within the organizational hierarchy. This omission was purposefully intended, rather than established through oversight, because the primary intent of this dissertation is to examine innovative decision-making in organizations in terms of program and policy alternatives. Secondly, organizational structure is excluded from the scope of decision-making intentionally, because structural variables are the independent variables manipulated by the researcher in the innovation model simulation. Thirdly, choices in the organizational choice structure are assumed to be non-conflictual in nature and to fall within the broad legislative mandate of the public agency. Hence, choices in the choice structure all represent potentially acceptable bureau choices, and administrative discretion, exercised through the decision-making process, determines which of the potential choices is actually implemented at any point in time. Choices are exclusive in three respects. The same resource unit cannot be expanded simultaneously on two different choices, causing a choice to have exclusive claim over any organizational resource unit allocated to it at that point in time. The attention of any organizational member cannot be devoted simultaneously to two different choices, causing a choice to have the exclusive attention or recommendation of any individual within the organization at any point in time. Also, since choices are defined within the innovation model in terms of benefit-cost ratio, payoff, costs, and risk, only one choice can represent the status quo at any point in time.

The number of organizational decisions in any time period consists of a one-to-one mapping with the number of authoritative individuals in the organization capable of committing organizational resources. Therefore it is possible for one organization to have made a higher absolute number of innovative choices over a given number of time periods than another organization, and simultaneously to experience a lower percentage of total authoritative decisions which are innovative. To provide this data and other types of information, we shall output five dependent variables from the innovation model simulation: the number of attempted innovations which were not successfully adopted, the percentage of innovations are of total authoritative decisions made, total organizational resources, and organizational slack. Each of these dependent variables are outputed every time period in any given run and are cumulative across time periods for any run.

Independent variables in the innovation model simulation are eight organizational variables: span of control, number of levels in the organization, degree of decentralization, organizational age, degree of hierarchy, number of choices available for potential scrutiny in the choice span, percent of organizational resources set aside as organizational slack, and the average amount of fixed costs of choices in the choice space. Each organizational variable has three levels—high, medium and low.

High, medium, and low values for each of the organizational variables are displayed in Table 1.

Table 1. High, Medium, and Low Values of the Innovation Model
         Simulation Organizational Variables

Organizational Variables	High	Medium	Low
Span of control	5	3	2
Number of levels	5	4	3
Decentralization	4	2	1
Organizational age	40	20	10
Hierarchy	100%	60%	10%
Number of choices	50	25	10
Percent slack	50%	20%	5%
Average choice sunk cost	50%	15%	0%

A span of control as low as 2 would most likely be found in
organizations engaging in research; a span of control of 3, or
a medium span is more typical of program analysis and execution
units; a high span of control or 5 would exemplify public
agencies where the work is fairly routine and client interactions
are specified, such as teams of bank examiners, safety inspectors,
highway field offices, and some types of casework.

Organizations with a low number of levels would be typical of
research organizations, special trouble shooting units, and high
priority problem-solving units. A medium number of levels of 4
could most likely be found in regulatory agencies. When concrete
goods are produced, as in the defense policy area, or specific
services are delivered to clients, as in the case of welfare or
social security, the number of levels is likely to increase to 5
or more.

When decentralization is very low, only the top person in the
organizational hierarchy can commit organizational resources to an
innovative alternative; the President committing U.S. troops in
defensive actions abroad is an illustration of this low degree of
decentralization. Agency heads testifying before legislative
committees or bodies and committing, through their testimony,
their agencies to specific actions, is a second illustration of
low decentralization. Low decentralization usually occurs in
situations of crises and stress. Consequently, organizations
which perceive themselves to be under perpetual crises and stress,
such as intelligence agencies, tend to have a low degree of
decentralization. Medium decentralization, or inclusion of at
least a second level of authoritative individuals is more typical
of government agencies. High decentralization occurs primarily
in research organizations and agencies with significant contract
authority where, for all practical purposes, individuals with the

52

most technical expertise in a specific policy area approve resource spending decisions.

In the innovation model, the length of time period is abstract and non-specific. However, we might argue that a simulated time period could represent a year in the life of a public agency. Hence, the manpower and poverty organizations established in the sixties would be examples of young organizations, while the New Deal organizations established after the depression would be considered comparatively old organizations. A twenty year old public agency would be considered well past youth and into middle-age.

Hierarchy, as defined within the context of the innovation model simulation, is the probability that a superior will consult his or her subordinates in any given decision situation. In a completely non-hierarchical organization, superiors would consult their subordinates in most decision situations. This is most likely to occur in organizations where the technology is complex, task specialization is high, and the criteria for policy evaluation are multi-faceted or non-specific. In a very hierarchical organization, subordinates would never be consulted by their superiors. This situation would most likely occur where the technology is not complex, where the task to be accomplished in routine, and where the supervisor feels little need to rely on the technical expertise of his or her subordinates.

The number of choices available to a public agency may depend on many things, including the number of organizational goals established in authorizing legislation, the scope of the legislative mandate, and the state of technology in the policy area of organizational concern. If the authorizing legislation established multiple organizational goals, the number of choices available to the agency is greater than if there is no diversification of purpose and the legislation establishes only one goal. If the legislative mandate is broad in scope, or the interpretation of the legislative mandate is broad in scope, then the number of choices potentially available to the public agency is broader than if the interpretation is narrow or the mandate very restrictive. Should the policy area of concern to the organization have a complex technology, the alternatives will be greater than if the technology is simple.

The percentage of total agency resources which an organization can devote to non-specific purposes and non-directed activities depends on the success with which the organization is meeting its mandated goals, or its ability to ignore the achievement of mandated goals without sanctions. Organizations with clearly defined tasks where measurement of success attains some degree of consensus are more likely to perceive excess resources or slack than organizations where task definement is not clear and success criteria are not established.

53

The ratio of choice sunk costs to choice total costs may largely depend on the need to acquire capital equipment and fixed assets in order to implement an alternative. In policy areas where a complex technology requires much additional capital equipment or considerable outside consulting, sunk costs will be comparatively higher than when capital equipment and outside consulting requirements are low. Organizations with diversified personnel and comparatively high amounts of in-house hardware will more likely experience a lower choice sunk cost to choice total cost ratio than organizations without these in-house capabilities.

As noted earlier, the innovation model simulation is probabilistic rather than deterministic, relying partially on random distributions. For this reason, one run at each level of an organizational variable is not sufficient to test the effect of one level versus another level. Rather, we shall conduct twenty runs at each level of each organizational variable and average the dependent variable results for the twenty runs. When one organizational variable is being tested, the remaining seven organizational variables are fixed at their respective medium level values for that set of runs to minimize the effect of the seven variables not being tested on the dependent variable results. Each run, except when testing for oganizational age, shall consist of twenty time periods. The numbers twenty in both cases were arbitrarily selected as being sufficiently small to offer economy of computer resources yet sufficiently large to give a distributional average. We shall use difference of means tests and simple regression analysis to examine our results. We are interested in two things primarily: significant differences in the dependent variables when various levels of the independent variables are tested, and significant differences in the rates of increase of the dependent variables when various levels of the independent variables are tested. In essence, sensitivity testing shall be conducted, by varying one of the eight organizational structural variables at a time. The results of a set of runs where one and only one of the organizational structural variables has been set at a low value, with all other organizational structural variables set at a medium level, will be compared with the results of both a set of runs where that same variable has been set at a high level, with all other variables set at medium, and with a set of runs for a standard organization. In a standard organization, all independent variables are fixed at medium values for the duration of the set of runs. In this manner we can determine model sensitivity, and presumably real world organizational sensitivity, to changes in organizational structure, insofar as organizational innovation is concerned. The student's t statistic shall be used in the difference of means test to determine significant differences in the dependent variables when various levels of the independent variables are tested, and also in the difference of beta coefficients test to determine significant differences in the rates of increase of the dependent variables when various levels of the independent variables are tested. In the latter case, dependent variables shall be expressed in terms of cumulative period means for a set of runs. Since there is some danger in a series of t tests of experiencing some random or chance significance, we shall place particular emphasis on any organizational structure variables resulting in very high t values, since a high t value reduces the possibility of random significance.

At the beginning of each run, a new organization is set up through the following processes. First, the program, given the number of levels in the organization and the span of control, determines the total number of individuals who are organizational members. With a random number generator with a uniform distribution, each individual is then given three numbers varying between one and ten--a risk factor indicating his or her willingness to take calculated risks, a number of resource units he or she can expend in search for innovative alternatives, and a dissatisfaction measure which consists of three components. The three components of the dissatisfaction measure are a random factor, a factor determined by whether or not the innovation the individual suggested in the previous time period was attempted, and a factor determined by whether or not the innovation he or she suggested in the previous time period was successfully adopted. A uniform distribution is used for dissatisfaction and the other factors since the model includes no assumptions which would provide a basis for skewing the distributions to either tail, or for normalizing them. A uniform distribution provides equal probability of any number in the range of interest being generated. Initially, in the first time period the entire dissatisfaction measure is set randomly, since the individual at that time has no previous record of recommendation acceptance by authoritative members of the organizational hierarchy. Subsequently, the random component is reset every time period in recognition of the fact that factors external to the organization may partially determine his or her dissatisfaction with the status quo. The second component of the dissatisfaction measure is decreased by one each time the organization attempts an innovation recommended by the individual in question in the previous four time periods; this algorithm recognizes that an individual is likely to have his or her dissatisfaction with the status quo reduced if authoritative individuals are listening to and acting upon his or her recommendations. The third component of the dissatisfaction measure is decreased by one each time an innovation recommended by the individual in question in the previous four time periods is successfully adopted, in recognition of a likely further lowering of the individual's dissatisfaction if his or her suggestions are actually enacted.

55

At the beginning of each run, choices in a choice space are also established by the assignment of four values. Three numbers are randomly generated between one and ten which represent a risk factor indicating the probability that an innovation, if attempted, will be successfully adopted, a payoff factor or the amount by which the organization's resources (minus costs) will be increased if the innovation is successfully adopted, and a total cost measure or the amount by which the organizations resources will be reduced if the innovation is attempted. Sunk or startup costs are derived as a percentage of total costs.

As soon as these initial procedures are enacted, the program begins a twenty time period run, completing the two major algorithms described earlier in sequence twenty times each. Now let us turn to some hypotheses abut the impact of the independent organizational variables on ur dependent variables, and explore some of our findings.

FLOW-CHART OF ONE TIME PERIOD   i = individual
                                       o = organization

Stage I

Individuals pick
recommendations

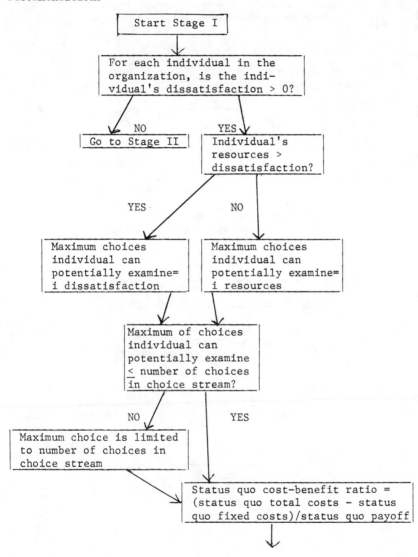

57

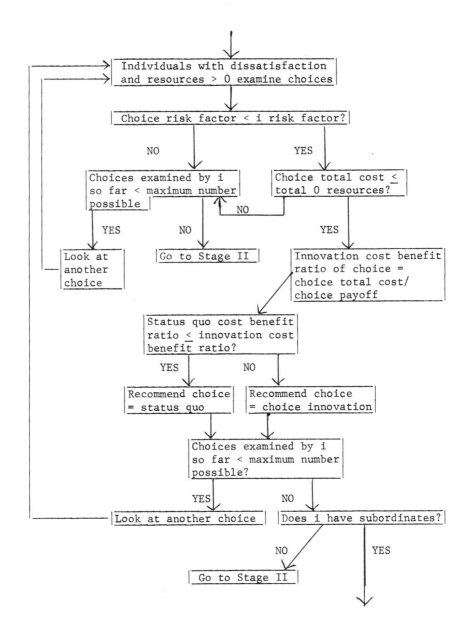

Individuals with dissatisfaction
and resources > 0 examine choices

Choice risk factor < i risk factor?

NO

YES

Choices examined by i
so far < maximum number
possible

Choice total cost ≤
total 0 resources?

NO

YES

NO

YES

Look at
another
choice

Go to Stage II

Innovation cost benefit
ratio of choice =
choice total cost/
choice payoff

Status quo cost benefit
ratio ≤ innovation cost
benefit ratio?

YES

NO

Recommend choice
= status quo

Recommend choice
= choice innovation

Choices examined by i
so far < maximum number
possible?

YES

NO

Look at another choice

Does i have subordinates?

NO

YES

Go to Stage II

58

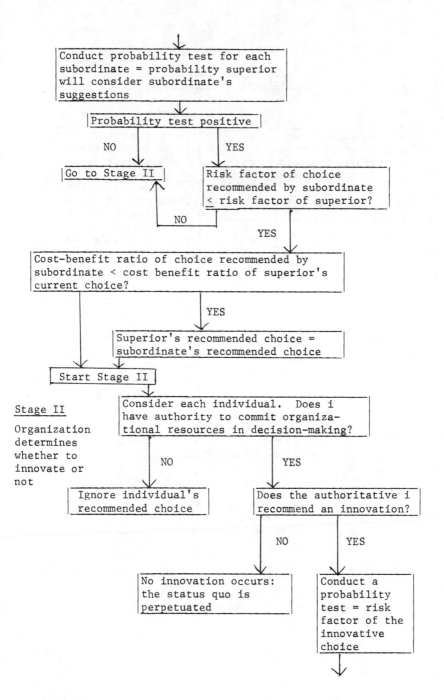

↓

Conduct probability test for each
subordinate = probability superior
will consider subordinate's
suggestions

↓

Probability test positive

NO   YES

Go to Stage II   Risk factor of choice
                        recommended by subordinate
                        ≤ risk factor of superior?

NO

                        YES

Cost-benefit ratio of choice recommended by
subordinate < cost benefit ratio of superior's
current choice?

YES

Superior's recommended choice =
subordinate's recommended choice

Start Stage II

Stage II   Consider each individual. Does i
                    have authority to commit organiza-
Organization   tional resources in decision-making?
determines
whether to
innovate or   NO   YES
not

        Ignore individual's   Does the authoritative i
        recommended choice   recommend an innovation?

                            NO   YES

                No innovation occurs: Conduct a
                the status quo is   probability
                perpetuated   test = risk
                                           factor of the
                                           innovative
                                           choice

                                            ↓

59

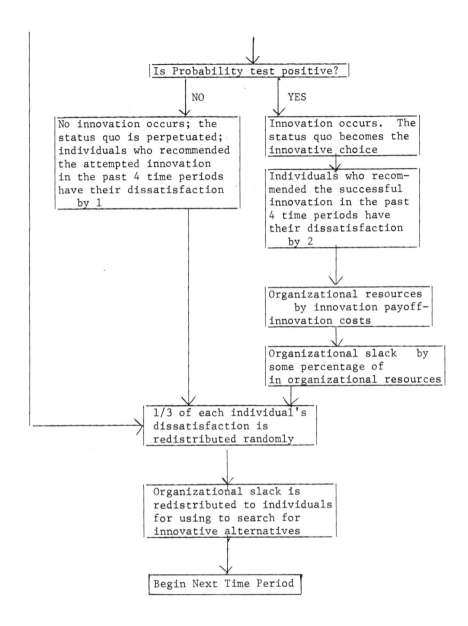

CHAPTER FIVE

Hypotheses and Findings

Hypotheses About the Number of Innovations:

A primary intent of this innovation model simulation is to
determine the impact of various organizational variables--inde-
pendent variables in this research context--on the number of
innovations an organization successfully adopts in a given number
of time periods. Drawing from the literature when it is applicable, we shall develop operational hypotheses about the impact
of our organizational variables on the amount of innovation in
which an organization engages.

Span of Control:

While there is no direct test of the effect of low and high
spans of control on organizational innovation in the literature,
there are several references to the detrimental effect of tight
central control on innovative processes. Pelz and Andrews, in a
laboratory situation with scientists and engineers as subjects,
found that the creative abilities of their subjects were enhanced
when individuals worked on particular specialities as main projects for relatively short periods, where co-ordination was loose,
where there was an opportunity to influence decision-makers, and
where there were good methods for communicating ideas.[1] Corwin
found in a study of forty-two cooperating public schools and ten
universities with Teacher Corp programs that innovativeness, as
measured by the number of new technologies introduced in the
school through the Teacher Corp program, was related to the
organizational control exercised by the school. However, whether
high span of control or low span of control implies greater
organizational control is not immediately evident. Arguments can
be made for both positions. On the one hand, it can be argued
that high span of control implies less time on the part of the
supervisor to devote to each subordinate and therefore, less time
to interfere with innovative action in which the subordinate
engages and to monitor and check his or her performance. On the
other hand, it can be argued that low span of control implies
greater time on the part of the supervisor allocated to consider-
ation of subordinates' ideas and to interaction and communication
with subordinates. Since a low span of control is more frequently
connected in the real world with high complexity of task, and
since we might argue that tasks of high complexity provide a
greater lattitude for innovation than do tasks of low complexity,
we shall accept the latter argument here:

61

Hypothesis 1:   Organizations with high span of control will
                   adopt successfully fewer innovative alternatives
                   than organizations with low span of control.

Hypothesis 1A: Organizations with medium span of control will
                   adopt successfully fewer innovative alternatives
                   than organizations with low span of control.

Hypothesis 1B: Organizations with medium span of control will
                   adopt successfully more innovative alternatives
                   than organizations with high span of control.

Findings About the Impact of Span of Control on Number of Innovations:

For each test of a hypothesis, a set of twenty runs was
conducted. The mean number of innovations in the last time period
was obtained and difference of means tests were conducted. The
results of hypotheses about the impact of organizational variables
on number of innovations are displayed in Table 5-1.

Innovation means for high, medium, and low span of control
are 4.667, 3.000, and 3.667 respectively. We find that the number
of innovations occurring under high span of control exceeds the
number of innovations occurring under low span of control, which
is the reverse ordering of that in hypothesis 1; our difference
of means test reveals that this difference is insignificant at the
.05 level, implying that there is little difference between innovation occurrence under high span of control and low span of
control. In hypothesis 1A, we expect medium span of control to
result in fewer innovations than low span of control. The data
do bear out our expectations, but again, we find the difference
between medium and low span of control to be insignificant. In
hypothesis 1B, we contended that medium span of control would
result in more innovation than high span of control, the exact
opposite of the data results. This difference is significant
when a difference of means test is employed. Hence, the data do
not confirm any of the first set of hypotheses.

Span of control has little impact on number of innovations.
While research organizations have low spans of control, we must
conclude that any innovativeness exhibited by this type of organization is induced or facilitated by phenomena other than span
of control. Similarly, while factories and mass production
organizations generally have higher spans of control, any paucity
of innovation does not appear to be generated by the average
number of workers directed by one supervisor.

Number of Levels of Organization:

Again, there are no direct tests in the literature of the effect of number of levels of organization. Both span of control and the number of levels of organization are major structural features of any agency, however, and for this reason are worthy of inquiry into the nature of their impact on number of innovations. We could argue that an organization with fewer levels would have fewer points through which red tape and regulations could stifle communications and serve as a veto point for new ideas. Number of levels of organization is one measure of size; ceteris paribus, an organization with more levels is a bigger organization than one with fewer levels. Mueller proposes that organizational size will have little effect on organizational innovativeness as a result of his case study of the discovery of nylon at Dupont.[3] However, Hage and Aiken, after studying sixteen social welfare agencies over a five year period, posit a negative relationship between innovativeness and organizational size.[4] Drawing from their study, we propose:

Hypothesis 2:   Organizations with a high number of levels will adopt successfully fewer innovative alternatives than organizations with a low number of levels.

Hypothesis 2A: Organizations with a medium number of levels will adopt successfully fewer innovative alternatives than organizations with a low number of levels.

Hypothesis 2B: Organizations with a medium number of levels will adopt successfully fewer innovative alternatives than organizations with a low number of levels.

Findings About the Impact of Number of Levels of Organization on Number of Innovations:

Very little variation is exhibited in the number of innovations successfully adopted when we test for high, medium, and low levels of organization. In the simulation, organizations with a high number of levels adopted a mean of 2.954 innovations; organizations with a medium number of levels a mean of 3.000 innovations; and organizations with a low number of levels a means of 3.682 innovations. Since we hypothesized that organizations with a low number of levels would adopt successfully more innovations than either organizations with medium or high numbers of levels, our expectations are fulfilled by the simulation results. Similarly, we expected organizations with medium numbers of levels to adopt more innovations than organizations with low number of levels, and the simulation results support this. Differences of means test, however, show none of the expected results in the data to be significant. Hypothesis 2, 2A, and 2B are not confirmed by the innovation model simulation.

Number of levels appears to have little impact on the number of innovations successfully adopted by an organization. This aspect of organizational size is not an impediment to policy innovation nor a facilitator of policy innovation. This finding contradicts opponents of policy innovation. This finding contradicts opponents of big government who argue that an increase in organizational size will necessarily result in reels of red tape and a stultifying environment. Bureaucratic size, at least when measured in terms of number of levels in the hierarchy, cannot be faulted for the sometimes ponderous grinding of the administrative wheels.

Degree of Decentralization:

Here, degree of decentralization is indicated by the number of levels of organization, starting from the top, where individuals have the authority to make organizational decisions, thereby committing agency resources. A highly decentralized organization would have a greater number of levels of authoritative individuals than a lowly decentralization organization. In a highly decentralized organization, decisions would not have to flow upward as great a distance before receiving organizational action as they would in an organization with less decentralization. In the former organization, decision-making authority has been decentralized to lower levels.

While Thompson does not state directly that decentralized decision-making authority is positively related to organizational innovation, he does argue that bureaucratic hierarchial structure has a negative impact on innovation, an effect arising from a centralization of resources which presumably are a prerequisite to decision-making. He also argues that great concern on the part of individuals within the organization over the internal distribution of power is negatively related to innovativeness in achieving organizational goals. From this we might infer that in a decentralized organization where the distribution of power is more even than in a non-decentralized one, exhibited innovativeness will be greater.[5]

In their study of sixteen social welfare agencies, Hage and Aiken developed a centralization score based on the average degree of participation in the four decision-making areas of hiring personnel, promotion of personnel, adoption of new organizational policies, and adoption of new programs or services. Using partial correlations to control for spurious relationships, Hage and Aiken found that centralization among other structural and formalization variables had little impact on innovation. However, later, when the same authors find a moderate negative correlation between innovation and the performance variable satisfaction with expressive relations, they argue that the organizational conditions which facilitate the introduction of change, such as occupational diversity and decentralization, reduce individuals' satisfaction with their interpersonnal relationships because of the conflicts they stimulate.[6] Since Hage and Aiken seem so equivocal on this point, we shall draw primarily from Thompson for our next hypothesis:

Hypothesis 3: Organizations with highly decentralized decision-making authority will adopt successfully more innovative alternatives than organizations with low decentralization of decision-making authority.

Hypothesis 3A: Organizations with medium decentralization of decision-making authority will adopt successfully more innovative alternatives than organizations with low decentralization of decision-making authority.

Hypothesis 3B: Organizations with medium decentralization of decision-making authority will adopt successfully fewer innovative alternatives than organizations with high decentralization of decision-making authority.

Findings About the Impact of Degree of Decentralization on Number of Innovations:

High decentralization resulted in a mean innovation of 22.200. This is fourteen innovations above any other innovation mean. Medium decentralization resulted in a mean innovation of 3.000 and low decentralization resulted in a 0.550 mean innovation, the lowest of all innovation means. Clearly, the impact of degree of decentralization on the number of innovations successfully adopted by an agency is substantial. We hypothesized that a highly decentralized organization would result in more innovation than low decentralization. The data support all three hypotheses. Difference of means tests reveal all the hypothesized differences in amount of innovation to be significant. Hypotheses 3, 3A, and 3B are confirmed.

These findings tend to support the Thompson position which implies that a more equitable distribution of power within organizations results in greater policy innovations. Ironically, in most democratic countries which pride themselves on their acceptance and adherence to democratic principles, the predominant form of organization is bureaucratic and non-democratic. Consequently, most of the members of the labor force spend a substantial portion of their working lives in a work environment whose predominant principles contradict the principles by which the country is governed. Our innovation model simulation results imply that policy innovations could be increased in bureaucratic organizations by decentralizing decision-making power, thereby injecting wider individual participation and greater democracy into organizational decision-making.

Organizational Age:

Kaufman hypothesizes that age will have a positive effect on innovation since older organizations, according to him, must have developed an adaptive mechanism to survive.[7] Hage and Aiken find no relationship between the age of the welfare agencies they studied and organizational innovation.[8] However, from Downs, we may infer that age is inversely related to innovation. According to Downs, bureaus typically start as a result of the aggressive agitation and action of a small group of zealots through "spontaneous entrepreneurship."[9] With the advent of age, more formalized rule systems covering a wider range of possible situations are developed and zealots become less important than administrative officials. Expanded rules systems have the effect of making the behavior of parts of the organization more predictable to its other parts, of diverting the attention of officials from achieving the social functions of the bureau to conforming to the rules, and by increasing the bureau's structural complexity through greater sunk costs in current procedures, of strengthening organizational inertia. "Consequently, older bureaus tend to be more stable and less flexible than young ones."[10] While Downs contends, as does Kaufman, that the older a bureau is the less likely it is to die, unlike Kaufman, he does not equate long-lividness with flexibility and innovativeness. From Downs, we draw our next set of hypotheses:

Hypothesis 4:   An old organization will successfully adopt fewer innovative alternatives than a young organization.

Hypothesis 4A: A medium-aged organization will adopt successfully more innovative alternatives than an old organization.

Hypothesis 4B: A medium-aged organization will adopt successfully innovative alternatives than a young organization.

66

Findings About the Impact of Organizational Age on Number of Innovations:

In this set of hypotheses we focused on the impact of organizational age upon organizational innovation. Innovation means for old, medium-aged, and young organizations are 3.370, 3.000, and 3.25, respectively. In our model organizational age has little impact upon organizational innovation, for there is little variation in innovation means between sets of runs using varying numbers of time periods. Difference of means tests reveal none of the differences to be significant, causing a failure to confirm the significance of organizational age in determining the number of innovations successfully adopted.

Off-the-cuff wisdom jestingly has stated that governmental agencies should self-destruct in a fixed number of years because age brings stogginess, a tendency to continue fighting yesterday's problems today, strict adherence to nitpicking rules which undermine organizational purpose, and a lack of policy innovation. Our innovation model simulation data support this wisdom, or at least the portion which contends that the onset of organizational old age impedes further policy innovation. Essentially, we have found that there is no difference between the numbers of innovative alternatives successfully adopted by young organizations and the numbers of innovative alternatives successfully adopted by old organizations. Members of organizations which self-destruct after their youth need not worry, according to our results, about bold new courses of policy which the organization might have undertaken in middle and old age. The simulation results from the innovation model indicate that no such bold new actions would be in the making.

Degree of Hierarchy:

There appears to be a general consensus in the literature that rigid hierarchial structure diminishes innovation. Emphasis is placed on the need for openness and flexibility to accommodate innovative behavior. Open communication is one of the internal organizational inputs into the innovative process that Becker and Whisler found mentioned frequently in their survey of current theory and research of organizational innovation.[11] When focusing on the technological innovation of government agencies, Lambright[12] fixes on the significance of administrative pluralism. Thompson emphasizes the significance of diversity of inputs and structural looseness in the innovative process.[13] In a study by Evans and Black of factors associated with the success and failure of innovative staff proposals in business organizations, these authors found communication between line and staff played an important part in the adoption of innovative proposals.[14]

67

Hierarchy is defined here in terms of communication and rapport between subordinates and superiors. While other definitions of hierarchy may be valid, the impact of hierarchial structure on vertical communication and flows of information has frequently been noted. In an organization with a high degree of hierarchy, there is a low probability that superiors will consult subordinates in decision situations, since vertical information flows are restricted in this type of agency. By contrast, there is a high probability superiors will consult subordinates in an organization with a low degree of hierarchy and consequently less restrictive vertical information flows. From the literature we draw hypotheses about the impact of hierarchy on innovation:

Hypothesis 5:   Organizations with a high degree of hierarchy will adopt successfully fewer innovative alternatives than organizations with a low degree of hierarchy.

Hypothesis 5A: Organizations with a medium degree of hierarchy will adopt successfully fewer innovative alternatives than organizations with a low degree of hierarchy.

Hypothesis 5B: Organizations with a medium degree of hierarchy will adopt successfully more innovative alternatives than organizations with a high degree of hierarchy.

Findings About the Impact of Degree of Hierarchy on Number of Innovations:

Organizations with a high degree of hierarchy as we defined it within the context of this model--the probability of a superior consulting his subordinates in any given decision-situation--exhibit an innovation mean of 2.636. This is higher than the innovation mean exhibited by organizations with a low degree of hierarchy--1.762. This difference is neither great nor in the predicted direction. Both high and low degree of hierarchy means are lower than the innovation mean of 3.000 exhibited by organizations with a medium degree of hierarchy. None of the differences are significant, with the exception of the difference between medium and low degree of hierarchy means. However, this variation is not in the direction we predicted, so none of these three hypotheses is confirmed.

Degree of hierarchy in the innovation model simulation has very little impact on the number of innovations successfully adopted by an organization. Hence, supervisors may or may not consult their subordinates about potential policy innovations with little repercussions on the subsequent agency actions. This finding is not what we expected. We must keep two things in mind. First, the innovation model, by randomly distributing individual characteristics, makes no distinction between superiors and subordinates. Should superiors have substantially different individual characteristics from their subordinates, our finding about the impact of degree of hierarchy on number of innovations may no longer be valid. Secondly, superiors may wish to maintain a dialogue with subordinates for the purpose of upholding agency morale, creating a sense of self-importance, and other factors not included in this model.

Organizational Slack:

Organizational slack in this model is a certain percentage of the organization's total resource units distributed randomly to individual members to spend, if they choose, in the search for innovative alternatives. Hence, organizational slack is unused and uncommitted resources. Thompson defines slack as an objective-subjective ratio of the subjectively set aspiration levels to objectively determined achievement. When objective achievement exceeds the subjectively set aspiration level, Thompson argues that the impact of slack on organizational innovation is positive.[15] While our innovation model simulation does not employ Thompson's precise definition, we might argue that the implications of Thompson's concept are the same. If, under Thompson's specifications, objective achievement exceeds subjective goals, then presumably decision-makers within the organization will perceive excess resources uncommitted to on-going programs. Hence, we have the uncommitted resource situation assumed by the organizational slack definition employed in the innovation model simulation.

Thompson further argues that centralization of resources in the bureaucratic hierarchy is detrimental to innovation adoption. While he does not argue for any particular distribution of slack, the random distribution assumed by the innovation model is relatively decentralized in that the probability of any individual receiving a resource unit in any given time period is equal to the probability of any other individual receiving a resource unit, regardless of position in the organizational hierarchy. Overall, there is a higher probability that a greater number of resource units will accumulate at lower levels of the organization, since there are more individuals at lower levels. We might note that Thompson does not define his proposition about slack in terms of absolute amounts of resources, but rather ties his concept of slack to the relative resources and goals of the organization. Therefore we shall formulate our hypotheses about the impact of slack on innovation in terms of percentages, which are relative; more specifically, we shall formulate them in terms of the per centage slack constitutes of the total organizational resources:

69

Hypothesis 6:   Organizations with a high percentage of total
                 organizational resources uncommitted as slack will
                 adopt successfully more innovative alternatives
                 than organizations with a low percentage of total
                 organizational resources uncommitted as slack.

Hypothesis 6A: Organizations with a medium percentage of total
                 organizational resources uncommitted as slack will
                 adopt successfully more innovative alternatives
                 than organizations with a low percentage of total
                 organizational resources uncommitted as slack.

Hypothesis 6B: Organizations with a medium percentage of total
                 organizational resources uncommitted as slack will
                 adopt successfully fewer innovative alternatives
                 than organizations with a high percentage of total
                 organizational resources uncommitted as slack.

Findings About the Impact of Percentage Slack on Number of Innovations:

We hypothesized that organizations with a high percentage of total bureau resources devoted to slack would adopt successfully more innovative alternatives than organizations with a low percentage of total organizational resources devoted to slack. Since the former type of organization has an innovation mean of 2.900 and the latter an innovation mean of 2.650, the direction of variation we expected is borne out by the data. However, the variation does not appear to be very great, and, in fact, is not statistically significant at the .05 level. The innovation mean for a medium percentage of total organizational resources is 3.000. There is no statistically significant difference between high, medium, and low percentages of slack, causing us to fail to confirm hypotheses 6, 6A, and 6B.

This finding indicates that uncommitted resources alone, at least when distributed randomly among organizational members, is not sufficient to increase or decrease number of innovations substantially. This model conclusion contradicts literature suppositions that organizational slack impact significantly on the innovative process.

Number of Potential Choices:

No direct reference is made in the organization literature to the impact of the number of potential choices available to an organization on its innovativeness. James Q. Wilson contends that organizational diversity tends to support search for innovation.[16] Presumably, a diversified organization would have a greater range of organizational goals and consequently exhibit a

70

greater number of goal-approach behaviors. Each goal-approach
behavior could conceivably be modified, thereby causing such an
organization to have a greater number of potential choices, or
innovative alternatives potentially available in its choice space.
By contrast, an organization with little diversity would have a
limited range of organizational goals, a limited number of goal-
approach behaviors, and a smaller number of potential choices, or
innovative alternatives potentially available in its choice space.
Intuitively, the probability of an organization finding an innovative alternative more desirable than the status quo is higher the
greater the number of choices. Therefore, we hypothesize:

Hypothesis 7:   Organizations with a large number of choices
                 potentially available in their choice spaces will
                 adopt successfully more innovatives than organiza-
                 tions with a small number of choices potentially
                 available in their choice spaces.

Hypothesis 7A: Organizations with a medium number of choices
                 potentially available in their choice spaces will
                 adopt more innovative alternatives than organiza-
                 tions with a small number of choices potentially
                 available in their choice spaces.

Hypothesis 7B: Organizations with a medium number of choices
                 potentially available in their choice spaces will
                 adopt successfully fewer innovative alternatives
                 than organizations with a large number of choices
                 potentially available in their choice spaces.

Findings About the Impact of Number of Potential Choices on
    Number of Innovations:

     As we hypothesized, the innovation mean for organizations
with a large number of choices in their choice space, 2.818, is
greater than the innovation mean for organizations with a small
number of choices in their choice space, 0.1952. This difference
is statistically significant at the .05 level, causing us to confirm hypothesis 7. With an innovation mean of 3.000 for organizations with a medium number of choices in their choice space,
we find the data bear out the direction of variation predicted
in hypothesis 7A. This difference is also statistically significant at the .05 level, confirming hypothesis 7A. However, the
data do not manifest the direction of variation we predicted
between organizations with a medium number of choices and organizations with a high number of choices in hypothesis 7B. This
difference is not statistically significant at the .05 level.
The implications of the data are that increasing the number of
choices in the choice space of an organization results in
increased innovation up to a medium number of choices (twenty in

this simulation). Increasing the number of choices in the choice space of an organization beyond a medium number has little impact on organizational innovativeness.

Ratio of Choice Sunk Cost to Choice Total Cost:

From March and Simon we learn that sunk and innovation costs bias an organization toward the status quo.[17] We may assume that the greater the sunk costs the greater the bias:

Hypothesis 8:   Organizations whose potential choices have sunk costs which are a high percentage of total costs will adopt successfully fewer innovative alternatives than organizations whose potential choices have sunk costs which are a low percentage of total costs.

Hypothesis 8A: Organizations whose potential choices have sunk costs which are a medium percentage of total costs will adopt successfully fewer innovative alternatives than organizations whose potential choices have sunk costs which are a low percentage of total costs.

Hypothesis 8B: Organizations whose potential choices have sunk costs which are a medium percentage of total costs will adopt successfully more innovative alternatives than organizations whose potential choices have sunk costs which are a high percentage of total costs.

Findings About the Impact of Ratio of Choice Sunk Costs to Choice Total Costs on Number of Innovations:

When organizations face choices whose sunk costs are a high percentage of total costs, an innovation mean of 2.400 results. The simulation showed innovation means of 3.000 and 3.900 when organizations face choices whose sunk costs are a medium and low percentage of total costs. Since we hypothesized that high sunk costs would result in less innovation than low sunk costs, the data bear out our predictions. Hypothesis 8 is confirmed since this difference is significant at the .05 level. We also hypothesized that high sunk costs would result in less innovation than medium sunk costs, while medium sunk costs would result in less innovation than low sunk costs. Again, the data variation occurs as we expected. However, these two differences are not statistically significant so we cannot confirm hypotheses 8A and 8B. It appears that the differences in sunk costs must be large to result in significant differences in innovation level.

Interestingly, Table 5-1 shows that for four of the eight organizational variables tested by the innovation model simulation--specifically, number of levels, degree of hierarchy, percentage slack, and number of potential choices--the medium level of the variable in question produces or results in the highest amount of innovation. This suggests the possibility of a threshhold phenomenon, where increasing the magnitude of the independent variable beyond a medium level has little or no significant impact on the dependent variable number of innovations.

Table 5-1. Innovation Means and Standard Deviations

Variable Tested	Mean	Standard Deviation
Standard: (All variables set at medium values)	3.000	2.849
Span of Control:		
High	4.667	2.059
Low	3.667	2.869
Number of Levels:		
High	2.954	2.439
Low	3.682	2.589
Decentralization:		
High	22.200	24.319
Low	0.550	0.686
Organizational Age:		
Old	3.370	3.069
Young	3.250	2.325
Hierarchy:		
High	1.762	1.338
Low	2.636	2.237
Percentage Slack:		
High	2.900	1.889
Low	0.952	2.134
Number of Choices:		
High	2.818	1.500
Low	0.952	1.024
Choice Sunk Costs:		
High	2.400	0.821
Low	3.900	2.049

Table 5-2. Difference of Innovation Means Hypotheses Tests

Predicted Difference of Means	Computed Student's t	H_0 Rejected
Span of Control:		
low > high	-1.122	no
medium < low	-0.728	no
medium > high	-1.865	no
Number of Levels:		
low > high	0.855	no
medium < low	-0.793	no
medium > high	0.054	no
Decentralization:		
low < high	-3.879	yes
medium > low	3.644	yes
medium < high	-3.418	yes
Organizational Age:		
young > old	-0.136	no
medium < young	-0.269	no
medium > old	-0.385	no
Hierarchy:		
low > high	-1.473	no
medium < low	0.451	no
medium > high	1.750	no
Percentage Slack:		
low < high	-0.382	no
medium > low	0.429	no
medium < high	0.128	no
Number of Choices:		
low < high	-4.516	yes
medium > low	3.014	yes
medium < high	0.256	no
Choice Sunk Costs:		
low > high	4.189	yes
medium < low	-1.118	no
medium > high	0.882	no

$t_{.95,38} = \pm 1.686$

75

Table 5-3. Summary of Innovation Period Means
(rounded to two significant digits)

Period	Standard	Low Span of Control	High Span of Control	Low Number of Levels	High Number of Levels
1	1.75	1.81	3.00	1.91	1.73
2	2.30	2.67	4.20	3.00	2.55
3	2.65	2.95	4.53	3.48	2.77
4	2.90	3.24	4.67	3.57	2.83
5	3.00	3.38	4.67	3.61	2.95
6	3.00	3.48	4.67	3.61	2.95
7	3.00	3.52	4.67	3.61	2.95
8	3.00	3.57	4.67	3.61	2.95
9	3.00	3.62	4.67	3.61	2.95
10	3.00	3.67	4.67	3.61	2.95
11	3.00	3.67	4.67	3.61	2.95
12	3.00	3.67	4.67	3.61	2.95
13	3.00	3.67	4.67	3.61	2.95
14	3.00	3.67	4.67	3.61	2.95
15	3.00	3.67	4.67	3.61	2.95
16	3.00	3.67	4.67	3.61	2.95
17	3.00	3.67	4.67	3.61	2.95
18	3.00	3.67	4.67	3.61	2.95
19	3.00	3.67	4.67	3.61	2.95
20	3.00	3.67	4.67	3.61	2.95

Table 5-3. Continued

Period	Low Decentraliza-tion	High Decentraliza-tion	Low Degree of Hierarchy	High Degree of Hierarchy	Low No. of Choices
1	0.30	21.85	1.68	1.19	0.76
2	0.40	22.15	2.23	1.62	0.81
3	0.40	22.20	2.45	1.76	0.86
4	0.40	22.20	2.54	1.76	0.95
5	0.50	22.20	2.59	1.76	0.95
6	0.50	22.20	2.64	1.76	0.95
7	0.50	22.20	2.64	1.76	0.95
8	0.50	22.20	2.64	1.76	0.95
9	0.50	22.20	2.64	1.76	0.95
10	0.50	22.20	2.64	1.76	0.95
11	0.50	22.20	2.64	1.76	0.95
12	0.50	22.20	2.64	1.76	0.95
13	0.50	22.20	2.64	1.76	0.95
14	0.50	22.20	2.64	1.76	0.95
15	0.50	22.20	2.64	1.76	0.95
16	0.50	22.20	2.64	1.76	0.95
17	0.50	22.20	2.64	1.76	0.95
18	0.50	22.20	2.64	1.76	0.95
19	0.50	22.20	2.64	1.76	0.95
20	0.50	22.20	2.64	1.76	0.95

Table 5-3. Continued

Period	High No. of Choices	Low Percentage Slack	High Percentage Slack	Low Choice Sunk Costs	High Choice Sunk Costs
1	2.33	1.70	1.75	2.00	1.60
2	2.59	2.21	2.60	3.25	2.10
3	2.77	2.14	2.90	2.70	2.10
4	2.77	2.60	2.90	3.85	2.10
5	2.82	2.65	2.90	3.90	2.10
6	2.82	2.65	2.90	3.90	2.10
7	2.82	2.65	2.90	3.90	2.10
8	2.82	2.65	2.90	3.90	2.10
9	2.82	2.65	2.90	3.90	2.10
10	2.82	2.65	2.90	3.90	2.10
11	2.82	2.65	2.90	3.90	2.10
12	2.82	2.65	2.90	3.90	2.10
13	2.82	2.65	2.90	3.90	2.10
14	2.82	2.65	2.90	3.90	2.10
15	2.82	2.65	2.90	3.90	2.10
16	2.82	2.65	2.90	3.90	2.10
17	2.82	2.65	2.90	3.90	2.10
18	2.82	2.65	2.90	3.90	2.10
19	2.82	2.65	2.90	3.90	2.10
20	2.82	2.65	2.90	3.90	2.10

Table 5-3. Continued

Period	Young Age	Old Age	Period (continued)	Old Age (continued)
1	2.00	2.00	21	4.10
2	2.65	2.85	22	4.10
3	3.00	3.80	23	4.10
4	3.05	3.90	24	4.10
5	3.05	3.95	25	4.10
6	3.05	4.00	26	4.10
7	3.05	4.05	27	4.10
8	3.05	4.10	28	4.10
9	3.05	4.10	29	4.10
10	3.05	4.10	30	4.10
11		4.10	31	4.10
12		4.10	32	4.10
13		4.10	33	4.10
14		4.10	34	4.10
15		4.10	35	4.10
16		4.10	36	4.10
17		4.10	37	4.10
18		4.10	38	4.10
19		4.10	39	4.10
20		4.10	40	4.10

Chapter Five, Footnotes:

[1] Lloyd A. Rowe and William B. Boise, "Organizational Innovation: Current Research and Evolving Concepts," Public Administration Review, Vol. 34, No. 3, May-June, 1974, p. 287.

[2] Ronald G. Corwin, "Strategies for Organizational Innovation: An Empirical Conclusion," American Sociological Review, Vol. 37, No. 4, August 1972, p. 447.

[3] Willard F. Mueller, "A Case Study of Product Discovery and Innovation Costs," Southern Economic Journal, Vol. 24, No. 1, July 1957, p. 86.

[4] Jerald Hage and Michael Aiken, "Program Change and Organizational Properties: A Comparative Analysis," American Journal of Sociology, Vol. 72, March 1967, p. 509.

[5] Victor A. Thompson, Bureaucracy and Innovation (University of Alabama Press, 1969), p. 46.

[6] Hage and Aiken, p. 509.

[7] Herbert Kaufman, The Limits of Organizational Change (The University of Alabama Press, 1971), p. 100.

[8] Hage and Aiken, p. 509.

[9] Anthony Downs, Inside Bureaucracy (Boston: Little, Brown and Co., 1967), p. 5.

[10] Ibid., pp. 18-19.

[11] Selwyn W. Becker and Thomas L. Shisler, "The Innovative Organization: A Selective View of Current Theory and Research," The Journal of Business, Vol. 40, No. 4, Oct. 1967, pp. 462-469.

[12] W. Henry Lambright, "Government and Technological Innovation: Weather Modification as a Case in Point," Public Administration Review, Vol. 32, No. 1, Jan-Feb. 1972, p. 1.

[13] Rowe and Boise, p. 287.

[14] Ibid., p. 287.

[15] Thompson, p. 46.

[16] Rowe and Boise, p. 287.

[17] James G. March and Herbert A. Simon, Organizations (New York: John Wiley and Sons, Inc., 1958), p. 173.

CHAPTER SIX

More Findings

In the last chapter we found that decentralization and the type of choice structure an organization faces appear to have an impact upon organizational innovativeness. In this chapter we shall examine additional dependent variable results of the innovation model simulation.

Percentages of Innovation

The innovation model was established with a one-to-one correspondence between the number of organizational decisions occurring in any given time period and the number of authoritative individuals in the organization who were capable of making decisions to commit organizational resources to new alternatives. Every time period each authoritative individual makes an organizational decision by deciding whether or not to attempt an innovative alternative or to maintain the status quo. Hence, the number of organizational decisions made each time period varies to some extent with type of organization, as the number of authoritative individuals vary. Since the total number of decisions made by any organization is merely a summation of the number of decisions made in each time period, total number of decisions also varies to some extent by type of organization.

This variation in total number of organizational decisions made leads us to raise the question of whether or not organizations with a high number of innovations also have a high percentage of total organizational decisions made in favor of innovative alternatives over the status quo. Possibly organizations with high innovation have experienced this outcome because they are also organizations with high numbers of total organizational decisions each period. On the other hand, organizations with high numbers of total decision may innovate proportionately more, causing them instead to experience a high percentage of total decisions where innovation is favored over status quo maintenance. While the literature on organizational innovation does not speak specifically to this point, suppositions and findings about the impact of one organizational variable on innovativeness usually assume that other significant organizational variables are controlled. Consequently, we shall hypothesize here that organizational variables presumed to increase numbers of innovation will simultaneously result in a high percentage of total decisions where an innovative alternative is selected over the status quo.

81

The results pertaining to these hypotheses can be found in Table 6-2. The organizational variables which appear to cause an organization to exhibit a high innovation mean are not the same variables which appear to cause an agency to favor innovations over the status quo a high percent of decisions, with the exception of number of choices potentially available to the agency in its choice structure. Organizational variables impacting significantly on innovation means are degree of decentralization, ratio of choice sunk costs to choice fixed costs, and number of choices potentially available to the bureau. Organizational variables impacting significantly on innovation percentages are organizational age, degree of hierarchy, and number of choices potentially available.

Concerning organizational age, young organizations have fewer total decisions than do old organizations. Since we found in Chapter Five that there was no substantial difference between the numbers of innovations adopted by the two types of agencies, we are not surprised here to discover that innovations are adopted in a higher percentage of the total decisions of young organizations than of old organizations. However, the number of total decisions made in a twenty period time span is the same for organizations with high degree of hierarchy as for organizations with low degree of hierarchy. Similarly, there is no difference between the number of total organizational decisions made by organizations with a high number of choices potentially available and organizations with a low number of choices potentially available. The high percentage of innovation adoption by organizations with a high number of choices potentially available may result from a number of decisions being held constant and a greater number of innovation adoptions by this type of agency than for agencies with a low number of choices potentially available. In the case of degree of hierarchy, the difference between the number of innovations adopted by organizations with a high degree of hierarchy and the number of innovations adopted by organizations with a low degree of hierarchy is not statistically significant; however, apparently this variation is great enough to cause a significant difference in the percentage of innovation adoptions of the two types of agencies.

The findings about the impact of degree of decentralization on percentage of innovation adoptions are interesting. We may recall that degree of decentralization had a substantial impact on the number of innovations adopted. Due to decentralized decision-making authority, organizations with a high degree of decentralization have the largest number of organizational decisions being made in a twenty time period span. Here, we find that no substantial difference exists between the innovation percentage of highly decentralized organizations and that of lowly decentralized organizations. From this, we can infer that

82

the dramatic increase in total number of organizational decisions made by organization with high degree of decentralization contributes greatly to the equally dramatic increase in the number of innovations adopted by this type of agency. We may conclude that organizational variables resulting in high numbers of innovation adoption do not necessarily result in high percentages of innovation adoption; only when the total number of organizational decisions is held constant is the simultaneous occurrence of high numbers and high percentages of innovation adoption very probable.

The Differential Impact of Organizational Variables Having A Significant Effect on Organizational Innovation:

Organizational managers anxious to have innovative agencies may be limited in the number of structural changes which they can undertake in any given time span. In the public sector, legislative control over executive agency organization and reorganization is a major source of limitation. Civil service and merit systems provide another source of limitation. The inability of public managers to significantly expand or shrink agency goals, purposes, and mandates is a third source of limitation. Consequently, public managers with a limited operational sphere who, nonetheless, desire to increase agency innovativeness, may wonder what is an appropriate strategy to modify organizational structural variables. Does it matter in terms of marginal increases in innovativeness which structural change is sought first?

Having discovered which organizational variables within the framework of the innovation model have a significant effect on organizational innovation, we might wonder if the impact of one organizational variable is greater than the impact of another organizational variable. We may recall that the innovation means for high decentralization, low choice sunk costs, and high number of choices were 22.200, 3.900, and 2.818, respectively. The means for low decentralization, low number of choices, and high choice sunk costs were 0.550, 0.952, and 2.400, respectively. The innovation means appear to exhibit substantial variation. Table 6-2 displays hypotheses that the magnitude between the innovation means of these organizations, where one organizational variable found to impact significantly on innovation is set at its high level and all other organizational variables are set at their medium levels, is indeed, significant.

The findings about these hypotheses are also displayed in Table 6-3. The differences between innovation means of organizations with high decentralization and medium choice sunk costs, and agencies with low choice sunk costs and medium decentralization; organizations with high decentralization and medium number of choices, and agencies with high number of choices and medium decentralization; and organizations with low choice sunk costs

83

and medium number of choices, and agencies with high number of
choices and medium choice sunk costs are all significant. This
indicates that a public manager interested in achieving the
largest possible marginal increase in number of innovation adoptions per structural change would first decentralize his or her
organization. Secondly, he or she would seek out potential
choices with low sunk costs. Thirdly, he or she would seek to
increase the number of choices potentially available.

Number of Attempted Innovations:

Attempted innovation, within the context of the innovation
model, is not the sum of all innovations attempted, whether
successful or not, but rather is only those innovations which the
organization attempted and failed to adopt. In the innovation
model simulation, an innovation may be attempted and not successfully adopted when the probability test for innovation adoption
success is negative. The probability of failure in this test is
equal to the risk factor of the choice attempted. The probability
test simulates environmental forces which determine differential
riskiness of choices, and the success or failure of innovation
adoption, given differential risks. The literature says little
about attempted innovations, as we have defined the concept here.
Sometimes the literature is unclear about whether discussions of
organizational innovativeness refer to successfully implemented
innovations or to the universe of innovations, both successfully
implemented and attempted. We shall assume that the theoretical
literature about innovativeness refers to the universe of innovations and shall hypothesize here that organizational variables
assumed to increase the number of innovations successfully
adopted will simultaneously increase the number of innovations
attempted but not successfully adopted.

Table 6-5 displays hypotheses and findings about attempted
innovation. Organizational variables which impact significantly
on the number of attempted innovations are degree of decentralization, span of control, and the ratio of choice sunk costs to
choice total costs. Two of these organizational variables--degree
of decentralization and the ratio of choice sunk costs to choice
total costs--also impact significantly on the number of innovations successfully adopted by organizations. One organizational
variable which affects organizational innovation means which does
not affect attempted innovation means is the number of choices
potentially available in the agency's choice space. One organizational variable which affects organizational attempted innovation means but not organizational innovation means is span of
control.

Generally, factors which tend to increase numbers of innovation also tend to increase numbers of attempted innovation.

Implicit in this finding is the notion that the success rates for
the various types of organizations are very similar or the same.
Hence, organizational managers who encourage the development of
organizational structural variables which promote innovation
should expect a higher number of unsuccessful attempted innovations than organizational managers who are interested primarily
in maintaining the status quo.

Innovation Adoption Incidence Relative to Innovative
Failure Incidence:

In view of our last finding, is the promotion of innovation-
inducing factors "worth it" to the organizational manager? To
answer this question we shall consider whether the number of
innovation adoptions exceeds the number of innovation failures.
Here we are concerned about a comparison between the innovation
mean and the attempted innovation mean for any and each level of
each organization variable. Should the attempted innovation mean
significantly and repeatedly exceed the innovation mean, organizational managers could become psychologically battered and suffer
bruised egos. In addition, a high number of unsuccessful innovation attempts could drain organizational resources. We shall
hypothesize that the innovation mean for any given level of any
organizational variable shall exceed the attempted innovation mean.

In order to establish the reasonableness of the hypotheses in
Table 6-6, let us recall the organizational process algorithm of
the innovation model. We may remember that an organization under-
takes an innovative alternative when a person in a position of
authority discovers a choice, which, in addition to having a
benefit-cost ratio higher than that of the biased status quo ratio,
also has a choice risk factor equal to or less than the individual's risk factor. Disregarding the benefit-cost ratio calcula-
tion, let us focus on the effect of the risk factor. In order for
a high risk choice to be attempted, the following would have to
occur simultaneously:

1) the choice would have to have a high risk factor;
2) the individual must have a high risk factor; and
3) the individual must be in a position of authority and
   therefore capable of commiting organizational resources
   to innovative alternatives.

The probability of all three conditions being met simultaneously
is significantly less than the probability of two or one condition being met. Seemingly, fewer high risk choices will be
attempted than medium and low risk choices. The probability of
failure to successfully adopt a high risk choice is greater than
the probability of failure to successfully adopt a medium or low
risk choice, since the probability test determining success or

failure is weighted by the choice risk factor. This provides a
rationale for hypothesizing that innovation means will exceed
attempted innovation means.

The results of this set of hypotheses are found in Table 6-6.
Only three hypotheses in this set cannot be confirmed by the data
results of the innovation model simulation, while fourteen
hypotheses were confirmed. Hence, in fourteen different types of
organizations, we found that the number of innovations successfully adopted is greater than the number of innovations which
failed. Only in organizations with a low degree of decentralization, organizations with a high degree of hierarchy, and those
with a low number of potential choices in their choice spaces did
the number of innovations which failed not exhibit an incidence
significantly less than the number of innovations which were
successful. In each of these three types of organizations, the
incidence of number of innovations is very low, a fact which may
contribute the absence of significant differences between innovations and attempted innovations.

This finding is good news for organizational managers who are
interested in maximizing the innovativeness of their organizations.
Such managers can encourage factors which promote innovation with
little risk that the incidence of innovation failure will exceed
the incidence of innovation success. A further assurance that
innovation-conscious managers will not incur a greater number of
failures than successes is this: the only types of organizations
where there is a probability of innovation failures exeeding
successess are organizations which are non-innovation inducing.
Consequently, innovation-seeking managers operating under the
guidelines and by the decision rules of the innovation model can
continue their innovation-promoting activities, secure in the
knowledge that their egos will not be bruised and their hopes
shattered by repeatedly dismal failures. Here the old adage, "If
at first you don't succeed, try, try again," seems applicable.

Organizational Resources:

Organizational resources are very important to any type of
organization. Presumably an increase in resources in the form of
profit is the major if not the sole goal of private corporations.
With public bureaus we do not expect nor condone such single-
mindedness, but public agencies need adequate resources to achieve
goals established within the framework of the public policy-making
process. Consequently, we are interested in the extent to which
the organizational variables manipulated in the innovation model
simulation may impact upon total organizational resources.

Two lines of reasoning could be offered concerning the
impact of our organizational variables on total bureau resources.

We might argue that innovative organizations spend more resources on innovations which are not successfully adopted and hence, which do not pay off, than do non-innovative organizations. Consequently, the former type of bureau would be expected to have less total resources than the latter type of bureau. On the other hand, we have assumed that bureaus will innovate only when it is to their benefit to do so--that is, only when a higher rate of return will be incurred. Because innovative organizations, by definition, adopt more innovations than non-innovative organizations, they also more frequently adopt alternatives with higher rates of resource return. Consequently, one could argue that innovative organizations will accrue greater amounts of resources than non-innovative organizations. This is the argument we shall make here.

Generally, we shall hypothesize that organizational factors which increase innovativeness will also increase total bureau resources with four exceptions. We must acknowledge that initial model conditions may affect our outcomes, a fact for which we hope to control later by examining per capita means for the dependent variables. In particular, organizations with high span of control, high numbers of levels, and low percentage slack have higher initial total resources than organizations with low span of control, low numbers of levels, and high percentage slack. We would expect this initial state to influence our results by causing the former organizations to have higher total bureau resources at the end of twenty time periods than the latter. The fourth exception to the general rule is organizational age. Because old organizations have three times as long to accumulate resources than do young organizations, we will hypothesize that the total resources of the former organization will significantly exceed the latter.

The results for this set of hypotheses are displayed in Table 6-8. We find that span of control, number of levels, degree of decentralization, organizational age, and percentage slack, impact significantly in the predicted manner on total organizational resources. Three of these significant differences--those of span of control, number of levels, and percentage slack--may be due to initial model conditions. In the case of organizational age, old organizations do accumulate successfully more total bureau resources than young organizations. Degree of decentralization is the only organizational variable with a significant impact on total bureau resources. Highly decentralized organizations adopt more innovations than do lowly decentralized agencies; highly decentralized organizations also accumulate more bureau resources than do lowly decentralized agencies. Within the framework of the innovation model, there appears to be little correlation between factors which result in a high number of innovations and factors which result in a high amount of agency resources.

Per Capita Means:

When one level of one organizational variable was tested in the innovation model simulation, all other organizational variables were fixed at their medium level values for the duration of the test, so as to minimize the effect of the latter variables on the test data results. Theoretically, the organizational models used to test the high, medium, and low levels of the one organizational variable which was being examined were similar in all respects, with the exception of variation in the examined variable. In actuality, through no fault of the design, but rather through the logical impossibilities of maintaining total constancy, this was not the case. When one of the eight organizational variables we considered within the framework of this model was examined, the other seven were, in fact, held constant, but the total number of people in the organizations were allowed to vary by type of organization. For instance, if span of control is held constant, there will be more people in an organization with a high number of levels than a low number of levels. Similarly, if number of levels is held constant, there will be more people in an organization with high span of control than in an organization with low span of control. Since the amount of initial organizational resources is tied to the number of organizational members, we shall examine per capita means to investigate these possibly confounding effects.

We shall hypothesize that organizational factors presumed to increase numbers of innovation will also increase per capita innovation means. The results of this set of hypotheses can be found in Table 6-10. We find that number of levels in the organization, degree of decentralization, number of potential choices, and ratio of choice sunk costs to choice total costs influence per capita innovation in the predicted manner. Span of control also affects per capita innovation means significantly, but in a direction opposite that predicted; that is, high span of control, rather than a low span of control, results in significantly higher per capita innovation. Two of these organizational variables--span of control and number of levels in the organization--had little effect on the number of innovations. The other three--degree of decentralizaiton, number of potential choices, and ratio of choice sunk costs to choice total costs--effect both per capita innovation and numbers of innovation. The data show a greater number of significant differences between per capita innovation means than between non-per capita innovation means. With greater variation in the high and low input values for span of control and number of levels, these organizational variables might also impact significantly on number of innovations. Our hypothesis that organizational factors increasing total numbers of innovation will also increase per capita innovation is supported.

The data results on per capita attempted innovation are displayed in Table 6-12. We hypothesize that organizational factors presumed to increase numbers of attempted innovation will also increase per capita attempted innovation. Span of control, number of levels, degree of decentralization, and ratio of choice sunk costs to choice total costs--virtually the same line-up of organizational variables as those significantly affecting per capita innovation with the exception of number of potential choices--have a significant impact on per capita attempted innovation. Due to the possibly confounding effects of varying numbers of organizational members, we may have expected to find a greater number of significant differences between per capita attempted innovation means of different levels of organizational variables than between numbers of attempted innovation. In fact, there is only one organizational variable--number of levels--which significantly affects the former but not the latter.

An examination of per capita means is especially crucial for organizational resources. We may recall that initially in each set of runs, organizational resource units between zero and ten were randomly distributed to each organizational member. These resource units were then summed across individuals to derive organizational slack, which was then multiplied by a percentage to derive initial total bureau resources. Hence, we can see a direct linkage between initial total bureau resources and the number of individuals within the organization, merely as a consequence of technical model building, although one might argue that a similar rough correlation between number of organizational members and total bureau resources exists in the real world. We shall hypothesize that organizational factors presumed to increase innovation and organizational resources will also increase per capita bureau resources. An exception to this general hypothesis is organizational age. Because old organizations have three times as long to accumulate resource than young organizations, we shall contend that the per capita bureau resources mean for old organizations will be larger than the per capita bureau resource mean for young organizations.

The results for this set of hypotheses in Table 6-14 show that a span of control, number of levels, degree of decentralization, and organizational age, exhibit the predicted effect on per capita bureau resources. Percentage slack affects per capita bureau resources in a manner opposite that predicted, with the low percentage slack per capita bureau resource mean, a phenomenon which may be partially attributed to initial model conditions; only in the case of percentage slack is varying initial amounts of total organizational resources not directly attributable to varying numbers of organizational members. When the variation in number of organizational members is controlled by the use of per capita means, the impact of span of control and number of levels reverses. Earlier we found that high span of control and high numbers of levels resulted in significantly greater total bureau resources, an occurrence we attributed partially to the greater number of organizational members in these two types of organizations. Here we find that organizations with low numbers of levels, and agencies with low span of control have higher per capita bureau resource means. Generally, we may conclude that organizational factors presumed to increase organizational innovativeness also increase per capita bureau resources. We might argue that this occurs because innovative organizations, by virtue of selecting choices with more favorable benefit-cost ratios, experience a higher rate of return on their policy actions than do non-innovative organizations.

Rates of Change:

In order to monitor time trends in innovation, attempted innovation and organizational resources, public managers may be interested in rates of change. Hence, we shall look at rates of change of the simulation output variables. Specifically, we shall test to see if varying organizational input variables from high to low causes corresponding changes in the rates of change of the output variables. A lack of comment on this subject in the literature leaves us flexibility in hypothesis development. An argument could be made that factors presumed to increase inno- vation also increase rate of innovation and rate of attempted innovation. This argument assumes that innovative organizations not only adopt more innovations, but that they adopt innovations for a longer period of time. Similarly, we shall hypothesize that factors presumed to increase innovation also increase rate of resource change.

To operationalize rates of change, cumulative values for innovation were averaged across periods for each type of organiza- tion. An innovation mean, for example, was derived for period 1, period 2, etc. to the last period. This process was repeated for each level of each organizational variable. Then a simple regres- sion for each level of each organizational variable was conducted with time (period numbers) as the independent variable and the period innovation means as the dependent variable. Two sets of hypotheses and t-tests were then developed. One set determines whether or not the rate of change for one level of an organiza- tional variable differs in the above hypothesized manner from the rates of change for the other two levels of the organizational variable. This process of hypothesis development and testing was then replicated for attempted innovation and organizational resources.

Results for innovation rates of change hypotheses are dis- played in Table 6-15 and Table 6-16. We find that most, but not

90

all, of the various levels of our eight organizational variables resulted in positive innovation rates of change. Bureaus which did not incur positive innovation rates of change are organizations with a high number of levels, organizations with either high or low numbers of potential choices, and organizations with either high or low choice sunk costs. Interestingly, modification of an organization's choice structure results in high numbers of innovation but simultaneously does not generate positive innovation rates of change. While a substantial number of organizational factors do result in positive cumulative innovation rates of change, none of the beta coefficients are very large. Of the different types of organizations tested, any change in the cumulative innovation period means almost invariably occurs in the first five time periods, and frequently occurs in the first three or four time periods. Only organizations with low span of control and old organizations experience changes in cumulative innovation period means after the fifth time period, and these changes are very slight.

Very few of our hypotheses about significant differences in innovation rates of change of different levels of the same organizational variables were confirmed. In the cases of span of control and organizational age, we find the factor we presumed would increase innovation resulting in higher innovation rates of change did cause higher rates. However, our hypotheses about the impact of the six other organizational variables are not confirmed. Factors which were hypothesized to increase innovation do not necessarily increase innovation rates of change. Scanning the beta coefficients in Table 6-15, and the t-values in Table 6-16, we can see that generally, the rates of innovation change for different levels of most organizational variables do not differ substantially from one another. We may recall, for example, that decentralization, number of potential choices, and the ratio of choice sunk costs to choice total costs significantly affected the number of innovations adopted. None of these three organizational variables significantly affects innovation rates of change.

The implications of these findings are major. We have found that no organization innovates after its infancy, which may be slightly greater than five time periods as defined in the innovation model simulation, but usually is less than five time periods. Generally, the rates of change for all types of organizations are positive but low. We also found a lack of a significant relationship between a high number of innovations adopted successfully and innovation rate of change. Hence, organizational managers interested in maintaining an organizational state of innovativeness must do one of two things. They must constantly shift from one organization to another in order to be continually working for an infant organization, and therefore for the only type of organization where innovation occurs, or they must encourage their organi-

91

zations to self-destruct and be reformed periodically. Short of
organizational self-destruction, major re-organizations may
achieve the same purpose, although we did not directly test for
this within the framework of the innovation model simulation.

Organizational managers may fear continuing unsuccessful
attempts to innovate as a drain on the agency treasury. We can
determine whether this is a legitimate concern by examining
attempted innovation rates of change. We have hypothesized that
factors presumed to increase innovativeness will result in greater
rates of attempted innovation. The results concerning attempted
innovation are displayed in Table 6-17 and 6-18. Of the seventeen
types of organizations tested for positive betas, only roughly
half, or nine of the seventeen in fact, have positive rates of
attempted innovation change. Attempted innovation appears to
change even less than innovation. From this finding, we can
construe that public managers have little to fear from continuing
and draining unsuccessful innovation attempts. Organizational age
and number of potential choices affect attempted innovation rates
of change as predicted; span of control affects attempted innovation rate of change in a manner opposite that predicted. Of
these variables, only number of potential choices affected innovation significantly, creating little support for the assumption
that factors presumed to increase innovation simultaneously
increase innovation rates of change.

Under the assumption that innovative organizations exhibit
higher rates of return and therefore may accumulate more resources
than non-innovative organizations, we hypothesize that factors
presumed to increase innovativeness will result in higher resource
rates of change. The results for hypotheses about organizational
resources are found in Table 6-19 and Table 6-20. Table 6-19
shows that thirteen of the seventeen types of organizations tested
have positive rates of change. Generally, the betas are quite
high. A notable exception is the beta coefficient of 1.228 for a
standard organization, that is, an organization where all variables
have been set at their medium levels. This low beta coefficient
causes a curvilinear pattern where the high and low levels of
an organizational variable with the exception of degree of hierarchy exhibit higher rates of change than the medium level.
Apparently, moderate structural characteristics induce sluggish
changes in resources.

In Table 6-20, three organizational variables--decentraliza-
tion, age, and slack affect resource rates of change as predicted.
Span of control has an impact opposite that predicted. This provides moderate support for our supposition that factors presumed
to increase innovation will increase resource rates of change.
However, there appears to be little support for the supposition
that variables which significantly affect innovation also affect

92

resource rates of change, since decentralization is the only
variable affecting both. Hence, organizational managers under-
taking structural changes in their bureaus to increase innovativeness should not expect simultaneous increases in rates of resource
accumulation.

Table 6-1. Innovation Percentage means and Standard Deviations

Variable Tested	Mean	Standard Deviation
Standard: (All variables set at medium values)	0.0375	0.0356
Span of Control:		
High	0.0389	0.0394
Low	0.0611	0.0419
Number of Levels:		
High	0.0369	0.0305
Low	0.0450	0.0284
Decentralization:		
High	0.0278	0.0104
Low	0.0275	0.0343
Organizational Age:		
Old	0.0378	0.0810
Young	0.0800	0.0503
Hierarchy:		
High	0.0220	0.0170
Low	0.0329	0.0036
Percentage Slack:		
High	0.0363	0.0236
Low	0.0331	0.0283
Number of Choices:		
High	0.0352	0.0188
Low	0.0119	0.0128
Choice Sunk Costs:		
High	0.0263	0.1822
Low	0.0488	0.0256 ·

Table 6-2. Difference of Percentage Innovation Means Tests

Predicted Difference of Means	Computed Student's t	H_o Rejected
Span of Control:		
low > high	1.563	no
medium < low	-1.888	no
medium > high	-0.107	no
Number of Levels:		
low > high	0.366	no
medium < low	-0.844	no
medium > high	0.057	no
Decentralization:		
low < high	-0.342	no
medium > low	0.885	no
medium < high	1.141	no
Organizational Age:		
young > old	1.927	yes
medium < young	-3.014	no
medium > old	-0.015	yes
Hierarchy:		
low > high	-2.225	yes
medium < low	0.548	no
medium > high	1.802	yes
Percentage Slack:		
low < high	-0.381	no
medium > low	0.423	no
medium < high	0.122	no
Number of Choices:		
low < high	-4.481	yes
medium > low	3.122	yes
medium < high	0.258	no
Choice Sunk Costs:		
low > high	0.534	no
medium < low	-1.119	no
medium > high	0.352	no

$t_{.95,38} = \pm 1.686$

Table 6-3. Difference of Means Tests Between Variables Impacting
            Significantly on Innovation Means

Predicted Difference of Means	Computed Student's t	H_o Rejected
(high decentralization, medium choice costs) (low choice sunk costs, medium decentralization)	3.269	yes
(high decentralization, medium number of choices) (high number of choices, medium decentralization)	3.637	yes
(low choice sunk costs, medium number of choices) (high number of choices, medium choice sunk costs)	2.048	yes
(low decentralization, medium choice sunk costs) (high choice sunk costs, medium decentralization)	-7.537	yes
(low decentralization, medium number of choices) (low number of choices, medium decentralization)	-1.445	no
(high choice sunk costs, medium number of choices) (low number of choices medium choice sunk costs)	4.902	no

$t_{.94,40} = \pm 1.684$

Table 6-4. Attempted Innovation Means and Standard Deviations

Variable Tested	Mean	Standard Deviation
Standard: (All variables set at medium values)	1.450	1.432
Span of Control:		
High	3.133	1.302
Low	1.048	1.048
Number of Levels:		
High	1.273	1.077
Low	1.818	1.436
Decentralization:		
High	3.250	2.468
Low	1.250	1.410
Organizational Age:		
Old	1.370	1.387
Young	1.600	1.373
Hierarchy:		
High	1.191	1.289
Low	1.545	1.262
Percentage Slack:		
High	1.750	1.650
Low	1.250	1.651
Number of Choices:		
High	1.545	1.299
Low	1.095	0.944
Choice Sunk Costs:		
High	1.300	1.302
Low	2.250	1.773

Table 6-5. Difference of Attempted Innovation Means Tests

Predicted Difference of Means	Computed Student's t	H_o Rejected
Span of Control:		
low > high	−5.167	yes
medium < low	1.005	no
medium > high	−3.473	yes
Number of Levels:		
low > high	1.393	no
medium < low	−0.811	no
medium > high	0.445	no
Decentralization:		
low < high	−3.067	yes
medium > low	0.434	no
medium < high	4.201	yes
Organizational Age:		
young > old	0.514	no
medium < young	−0.330	no
medium > old	0.175	no
Hierarchy:		
low > high	−0.869	no
medium < low	−0.224	no
medium > high	0.595	no
Percentage Slack:		
low < high	−0.934	no
medium > low	0.399	no
medium < high	−0.599	no
Number of Choices:		
low < high	1.882	no
medium > low	−1.530	no
medium < high	0.341	no
Choice Sunk Costs:		
low > high	1.882	yes
medium < low	−1.530	no
medium > high	0.341	no

$t_{.95,38} = \pm 1.686$

Table 6-6. Hypotheses Tests of the Difference Between the
Innovation Mean and Attempted Innovation Mean
for Each Organizational Variable

Organizational Variable	Computed Student's t	H_o Rejected
Low Span	−3.835	yes
High Span	−2.355	yes
Low Level	−2.885	yes
High Level	−2.891	yes
Low Decentralization	1.946	no
Young Age	−2.664	yes
Old Age	−2.588	yes
Low Hierarchy	−1.946	yes
High Hierarchy	−1.375	no
Low Number of Choices	0.458	no
High Number of Choices	−2.939	yes
Low Percent Slack	−2.262	yes
High Percent Slack	−1.999	yes
Low Choice Sunk Costs	−2.654	yes
High Choice Sunk Costs	−3.115	yes
Standard (all variables set at medium)	−2.119	yes

$t_{.95,38} = \pm 1.686$

Predicted Difference of Means: Innovation Mean >
Attempted Innovation Mean

Table 6-7. Organizational Resource Means and Standard Deviations

Variable Tested	Mean	Standard Deviation
Standard: (All variables set at medium values)	3,444	465.784
Span of Control:		
High	8,716	1,618.720
Low	1,888	450.515
Humber of Levels:		
High	7,090	1,060.111
Low	2,248	1,010.318
Decentralization:		
High	13,098	7,040.193
Low	2,162	409.257
Organizational Age:		
High	4,728	1,056.336
Low	2,586	326.684
Hierarchy:		
High	3,599	832.831
Low	3,524	799.582
Percentage Slack:		
High	2,352	906.200
Low	9,362	2,961.312
Number of Choices:		
High	3,178	965.150
Low	2,773	1,724.621
Choice Sunk Costs:		
High	3,226	1,611.464
Low	3,311	1,027.208

Table 6-8. Difference of Organizational Resource Means Hypotheses Tests

Predicted Difference of Means	Computed Student's t	H_o Rejected
Span of Control:		
low < high	−17.843	yes
medium > low	10.605	yes
medium < high	−13.422	yes
Number of Levels:		
low < high	−15.152	yes
medium > low	4.730	yes
medium < high	−13.844	yes
Decentralization:		
low < high	−6.760	yes
medium > low	9.013	yes
medium < high	−5.964	yes
Organizational Age:		
young < old	−8.444	yes
medium > young	6.574	yes
medium < old	−4.848	yes
Hierarchy:		
low > high	0.287	no
medium < low	−0.382	no
medium > high	−0.713	no
Percentage Slack:		
low > high	23.448	yes
medium < low	−8.605	yes
medium > high	4.672	yes
Number of Choices:		
low < high	−0.910	no
medium > low	1.642	no
medium < high	1.094	no
Choice Sunk Costs:		
low > high	0.194	no
medium < low	0.514	no
medium > high	0.567	no

$t_{.95,38} = \pm 1.686$

Table 6-9.   Per Capita Innovation Means and Standard Deviations

Variable Tested	Mean	Standard Deviation
Standard: (All variables set at medium values)	0.075	0.07117
Span of Control:		
High	0.030	0.01319
Low	0.244	0.19129
Number of Levels:		
High	0.024	0.02015
Low	0.283	0.19916
Decentralization:		
High	0.555	0.04622
Low	0.014	0.01716
Organizational Age:		
Old	0.084	0.06653
Young	0.081	0.05814
Hierarchy:		
High	0.044	0.03345
Low	0.066	0.05593
Percentage Slack:		
High	0.073	0.04723
Low	0.066	0.05336
Number of Choices:		
High	0.070	0.03751
Low	0.024	0.02559
Choice Sunk Costs:		
High	0.060	0.02052
Low	0.097	0.05123

Table 6-10. Difference of Per Capita Innovation Means Hypotheses Tests

Predicted Difference of Means	Computed Student's t	H_o Rejected
Span of Control:		
low > high	4.214	no
medium < low	−3.631	no
medium > high	2.352	no
Number of Levels:		
low > high	5.925	yes
medium < low	−4.319	yes
medium > high	3.118	yes
Decentralization:		
low < high	−47.856	yes
medium > low	3.648	yes
medium < high	−24.653	yes
Organizational Age:		
young > old	−0.148	no
medium < young	−0.296	no
medium > old	−0.131	no
Hierarchy:		
low > high	−1.511	no
medium < low	0.451	no
medium > high	1.752	yes
Percentage Slack:		
low < high	−0.382	no
medium > low	0.429	no
medium < high	0.128	no
Number of Choices:		
low < high	−4.632	yes
medium > low	3.017	yes
medium < high	0.256	no
Choice Sunk Costs:		
low > high	2.962	yes
medium < low	−1.118	no
medium > high	0.883	no

$t_{.95,38} = \pm 1.686$

Table 6-11. Per Capita Attempted Innovation Means and Standard
           Deviations

Variable Tested	Mean	Standard Deviation
Standard: (all variables set at medium values)	0.036	0.03579
Span of Control: High Low	0.020 0.070	0.00834 0.06985
Number of Levels: High Low	0.011 0.140	0.00890 0.11042
Decentralization: High Low	0.081 0.031	0.06171 0.03523
Organizational Age: Old Young	0.034 0.040	0.03468 0.03432
Hierarchy: High Low	0.030 0.039	0.03223 0.03156
Percentage Slack: High Low	0.044 0.031	0.04126 0.04126
Number of Choices: High Low	0.039 0.027	0.03248 0.02359
Choice Sunk Costs: High Low	0.033 0.056	0.02012 0.04433

Table 6-12. Difference of Per Capita Attempted Innovation Means Hypotheses Tests

Predicted Difference of Means	Computed Student's t	H_o Rejected
Span of Control:		
low > high	2.668	yes
medium < low	−1.877	yes
medium > high	1.664	no
Number of Levels:		
low > high	5.351	yes
medium < low	−3.912	yes
medium > high	3.188	yes
Decentralization:		
low < high	−3.068	yes
medium > low	0.434	yes
medium < high	−2.751	yes
Organizational Age:		
young > old	1.209	no
medium < young	−0.329	no
medium > old	0.175	no
Hierarchy:		
low > high	−0.891	no
medium < low	−0.224	no
medium > high	0.596	no
Percentage Slack:		
low < high	−0.934	no
medium > low	0.399	no
medium < high	−0.599	no
Number of Choices:		
low < high	−1.265	no
medium > low	0.919	no
medium < high	−0.221	no
Choice Sunk Costs:		
low > high	2.126	yes
medium < low	−1.530	no
medium > high	0.398	no

$t_{.95,38} = \pm 1.686$

Table 6-13. Per Capita Organizational Resource Means and
            Standard Deviations

Variable Tested	Mean	Standard Deviation
Standard: (All variables set at medium values)	86.100	83.720
Span of Control:		
High	55.872	57.527
Low	125.866	30.034
Number of Levels:		
High	58.595	189.574
Low	172.923	166.129
Decentralization:		
High	327.450	313.824
Low	54.050	10.231
Organizational Age:		
Old	118.200	114.759
Young	64.650	62.876
Hierarchy:		
High	89.975	87.441
Low	88.100	85.315
Percentage Slack:		
High	58.800	56.782
Low	234.050	239.043
Number of Choices:		
High	79.450	76.771
Low	69.325	43.116
Choice Sunk Costs:		
High	80.650	10.287
Low	82.775	80.153

Table 6-14. Difference of Per Capita Organizational Resource
Means Hypotheses Tests

Predicted Difference of Means	Computed Student's t	H_o Rejected
Span of Control:		
low > high	1.811	yes
medium < low	-1.993	yes
medium > high	1.169	no
Number of Levels:		
low > high	2.078	yes
medium < low	-2.056	yes
medium > high	1.223	no
Decentralization:		
low < high	-3.795	yes
medium > high	1.656	no
medium < high	-3.239	yes
Organizational Age:		
young < old	-1.784	yes
medium > young	0.037	no
medium < old	-0.136	no
Hierarchy:		
low > high	0.069	no
medium < low	-0.075	no
medium > high	-0.136	no
Percentage Slack:		
low < high	3.109	no
medium > low	-2.546	no
medium < high	1.176	no
Number of Choices:		
low < high	0.103	no
medium > low	0.792	no
medium < high	0.262	no
Choice Sunk Costs:		
low > high	0.103	no
medium < low	0.125	no
medium > high	0.256	no

$t_{.95,38} = \pm 1.686$

Table 6-15. Innovation Rates of Change and Hypotheses Tests to Determine Betas Greater than Zero

Level Tested	Beta Values	Computed Student's t	H_o Rejected
Span of Control:			
High	0.0321	2.403	yes
Medium	0.0329	3.257	yes
Low	0.1164	2.847	yes
Number of Levels:			
High	0.0274	0.982	no
Medium	0.0329	3.257	yes
Low	0.0347	2.563	yes
Decentralization:			
High	0.0058	2.040	yes
Medium	0.0239	3.257	yes
Low	0.0064	3.908	yes
Organizational Age:			
Old	0.0152	7.152	yes
Medium	0.0329	3.257	yes
Young	0.1742	2.876	yes
Hierarchy:			
High	0.0096	2.025	yes
Medium	0.0329	3.257	yes
Low	0.0152	1.812	yes
Percentage Slack:			
High	0.0207	2.209	yes
Medium	0.0329	3.257	yes
Low	0.0315	8.964	yes
Number of Choices:			
High	−0.0022	−0.395	no
Medium	0.0329	3.257	yes
Low	0.0058	0.161	no
Choice Sunk Costs:			
High	−0.0511	−4.571	no
Medium	0.0329	3.257	yes
Low	0.0421	0.343	no

$t_{.95,38} = \pm 1.686$ x = Time (Period Number)

y = Innovation Period Cumulative Means

Table 6-16.   Innovation Rates of Change Difference of Beta
             Hypotheses Tests

Predicted Difference of Betas	Computed Student's t	H_o Rejected
Span of Control:		
low > high	1.959	yes
medium < low	-1.983	yes
medium > high	1.918	yes
Number of Levels:		
low > high	0.236	no
medium < low	-0.107	no
medium > high	0.222	no
Decentralization:		
low < high	0.020	no
medium > low	0.184	yes
medium < high	0.189	no
Organizational Age:		
young > old	5.453	yes
medium < young	1.377	yes
medium > old	0.193	yes
Hierarchy:		
low > high	-0.585	no
medium < low	1.344	no
medium > high	2.089	no
Percentage Slack:		
low < high	1.077	no
medium > low	0.130	no
medium < high	0.884	no
Number of Choices:		
low < high	0.219	no
medium > low	0.721	no
medium < high	3.038	no
Choice Sunk Costs:		
low > medium	0.757	no
medium < low	-0.067	no
medium > high	5.582	yes

$t_{.95,38} = \pm 1.686$

Table 6-17. Attempted Innovation Rates of Change and Hypotheses
Tests to Determine Betas Greater Than Zero

Level Tested	Beta Values	Computed Student's t	H_o Rejected
Span of Control:			
High	0.0263	2.367	yes
Medium	0.0096	0.390	no
Low	-0.0269	-0.337	no
Number of Levels:			
High	0.0092	0.315	no
Medium	0.0096	0.390	no
Low	0.0263	2.527	yes
Decentralization:			
High	0.0021	2.594	yes
Medium	0.0096	0.390	no
Low	0.0080	1.152	no
Organizational Age:			
Old	0.0020	2.095	yes
Medium	0.0096	0.390	no
Young	0.1034	2.247	yes
Hierarchy:			
High	0.0047	1.991	yes
Medium	0.0096	0.390	no
Low	-0.0171	-2.817	no
Percentage Slack:			
High	0.0088	0.665	no
Medium	0.0096	0.390	no
Low	0.1129	4.300	yes
Number of Choices:			
High	0.0061	1.774	yes
Medium	0.0096	0.390	no
Low	-0.1380	-2.915	no
Choice Sunk Costs:			
High	0.0119	1.337	no
Medium	0.0096	0.390	no
Low	0.0197	2.430	yes

$t_{.95,38} = \pm 1.686$

x = Time (Period Numbers)
y = Attempted Innovation Period
Cumulative Means

Table 6-18. Attempted Innovation Rates of Change Difference of
            Beta Hypotheses Tests

Predicted Difference of Betas	Computed Student's t	H_o Rejected
Span of Control:		
low > high	-2.485	no
medium < low	1.192	no
medium > high	-0.624	no
Number of Levels:		
low > high	0.166	no
medium < low	-0.182	no
medium > high	0.012	no
Decentralization:		
low < high	0.838	no
medium > low	0.081	no
medium < high	0.303	no
Organizational Age:		
young > old	4.604	yes
medium < young	-1.463	no
medium > old	0.380	no
Hierarchy:		
low > high	3.344	no
medium < low	1.056	no
medium > high	3.596	no
Percentage Slack:		
low < high	3.546	no
medium > low	-2.877	no
medium < high	0.029	no
Number of Choices:		
low < high	-4.416	yes
medium > low	3.630	yes
medium < high	0.140	no
Choice Sunk Costs:		
low > medium	0.646	no
medium < low	-0.336	no
medium > high	-0.091	no

$t_{.95,38} = \pm 1.686$

Table 6-19. Organizational Resource Rates of Change and Hypotheses
Tests to Determine Betas Greater Than Zero

Level Tested	Beta Values	Computed Student's t	H_o Rejected
Span of Control:			
High	16.996	30.741	yes
Medium	1.228	0.324	no
Low	6.965	2.840	yes
Number of Levels:			
High	15.587	0.316	no
Medium	1.228	0.324	no
Low	18.591	29.965	yes
Decentralization:			
High	410.415	4.425	yes
Medium	1.228	0.324	no
Low	2.603	4.504	yes
Organizational Age:			
Old	-186.784	6.185	yes
Medium	1.228	0.324	no
Young	1.077	0.934	no
Hierarchy:			
High	0.957	4.318	yes
Medium	1.228	0.324	no
Low	27.254	5.834	yes
Percentage Slack:			
High	42.734	29.181	yes
Medium	1.228	0.324	no
Low	-3.793	-5.572	no
Number of Choices:			
High	13.539	23.762	yes
Medium	1.228	0.324	no
Low	9.321	2.286	yes
Choice Sunk Costs:			
High	16.023	8.359	yes
Medium	1.228	0.324	no
Low	15.396	11.907	yes

$t_{.95,38} = \pm 1.686$

x = Time (Period Means)

y = Organizational Resource Period
Cumulative Means

112

Table 6-20. Organizational Resource Rates of Changes Difference
of Beta Hypotheses Tests

Predicted Difference of Betas	Computed Student's t	H_o Rejected
Span of Control:		
low > high	-3.989	no
medium < low	01.271	no
medium > high	-4.116	no
Number of Levels:		
low > high	0.060	no
medium < low	-4.520	no
medium > high	-0.344	no
Decentralization:		
low < high	-4.397	yes
medium > low	-0.478	no
medium < high	-4.408	yes
Organizational Age:		
young > old	3.322	yes
medium < young	0.032	yes
medium > old	1.869	no
Hierarchy:		
low > high	-5.632	yes
medium < low	-4.330	yes
medium > high	0.072	no
Percentage Slack:		
low < high	-28.809	yes
medium > low	1.304	no
medium < high	-10.214	yes
Number of Choices:		
low < high	-1.024	no
medium > low	-1.454	no
medium < high	-3.211	yes
Choice Sunk Costs:		
low > high	-0.271	no
medium < low	-3.537	yes
medium > high	-3.483	no

$t_{.95,38} = \pm 1.686$

113

CHAPTER SEVEN

Conclusions

The purpose of the innovation model simulation has been to present a formal theory of innovation and to examine the logical consequences of that theory. The formal theory of innovation presented here built upon the traditional rational choice model; the innovation model incorporates notions of rationality and a benefit-cost calculus used in selecting between various choices. To this basic format are added additional assumptions which delineate the status quo from innovation choices, and which establish principles whereby organizational members search for alternatives. The five additional assumptions are:

(1) An individual can review only a limited number of choices in any given time period.

(2) An individual's search for innovative alternatives is a direct function of his or her motivation and ability to engage in search activities. Motivation is directly related to the individual's dissatisfaction with the status quo; ability is directly related to the individual's access to slack resource units.

(3) Sunk costs bias the decision-maker toward the status quo.

(4) Payoffs from innovative choices contain an element of calculated risk.

(5) Organizational members have varying degrees of willingness to undertake calculated risks; an individual will only choose alternatives whose riskiness is equal to or less than his or her own willingness to take risks.

The innovation model consists of two basic algorithms: an in-individual process algorithm whereby the individual organizational member decides in each time period whether to recommend perpetuation of the status quo or adoption of a policy innovation, and an organizational process algorithm whereby authoritative individuals within the agency hierarchy decide what course of action the organization will pursue. The impact of eight organizational structural variables was tested on the following dependent variables: number of innovations, innovation adoption as a percentage of the total number of decisions made, number of attempted innovations, total organizational resources, per capita means, and rates of change. The innovation model includes random distributions and is therefore probabilistic or stochastic. To test for the impact of the model's independent variables on its dependent

variables, twenty runs of twenty time periods each were made for
each type of organization considered. Several conclusions emerge
from the innovation model simulation results. Let us examine each
of these conclusions and its impact in greater detail.

Public managers have an inherent interest in factors which
affect agency decision-making. Traditional organizational theory
is concerned with describing and prescribing organizational structure, primarily in terms of the consequences for efficient decision-making. Barnard, in his classic work on formal organizations,
delineates three executive functions: providing a system of communication, "promoting the securing of essential purpose," and
formulating and defining purpose.[1] Decisions about maintenance or
abolition of the status quo particularly involve the last two
executive functions. The decision itself and its implementation
is the process of "promoting the securing of essential efforts,"
to use Barnard's words. Efforts are essential when focused on the
maintenance of conditions conducive to organizational survival or
the achievement of organizational goals. Defining purpose involves
the process of choosing between various alternatives. Providing
a system of communication involves the process of developing the
internal structure of an agency. All three executive functions
are included in the innovation model, which may cause it to be of
some interest to public managers. We as researchers have controlled, manipulated, and varied organizational structure (the
communications and information network) in order to more closely
examine the effect of structure through decision-making (the
process of promoting essential efforts) on organizational
policies (innovation adoption).

Public managers who wish to promote policy innovation adoption within their agencies should focus on decentralization,
choice sunk costs, and the number of potential choices, according
to the data output from the innovation model simulation runs. Of
these three variables, the latter two are not discussed in any
detail by traditional organizational theorists. One might argue,
with some legitimacy, that choice sunk costs and number of
potential choices are not characteristics of formal organizational
structure, but rather are elements of the choice space in which
an agency operates by virtue of its legislative mandate.

Of the three variables having a significant effect on innovation adoption, decentralization has by far the greatest impact
and is the one of the three most directly controlled by the
manager. Considerable flexibility is granted to most higher level
public executives as to how much decision-making power they choose
to delegate to subordinates. In most public bureaus, executives
wishing to push decisions down to lower levels and to be informed
of the consequences of choices rather than being directly involved
in the decision process can do so. Similarly, through the culti-

116

vation of competing sources of information and the accumulation of
resources executives can closely guard their decision-making power,
delegating little of it to subordinates. The innovation-promoting
public executive will push decisions downward, encouraging subordinates to make choices for the organization at their own initia-
tive.

Public managers may find it more difficult as well as less
rewarding in terms of increases in innovation adoption to manipulate the choice structure. While executive influence over the
nature of the choice structure is more difficult to achieve,
primarily because changes in the choice structure require the
involvement of actors outside the agency rather than being mainly
an internal operation as in the case of decentralization, it is
nonetheless neither inconceivable nor impossible. In terms of
increases in the number of policy innovations adopted, organizations may find it slightly more rewarding to have a choice space
where average choice sunk costs are low than one where a large
number of potential choices are available.

Public managers may provide a choice space with low average
choice sunk costs by moving the agency into policy areas where
sunk costs and start-up costs are typically small. Expanding
agency policy areas requires either a willingness by top officials
to broadly interpret the existing legislative mandate or an agency
ability to secure a new legislative mandate.

Increasing the number of potential choices may require either
innovation developments within the general policy area under
agency jurisdiction, or a diversification of organizational purpose. The agency may be able to influence innovation developments
by directly funding or lobbying for government funding of research
and development activities in the field. Diversification of
organizational purpose would, again, require either a willingness
to interpret the original legislative mandate broadly, or an
ability to secure new authorizing legislation. Diversification
of organizational purpose would increase the number of choices
potentially available to a bureau by increasing the policy areas
of agency activity and thereby increasing the number of legitimate alternatives.

The innovation model results showed that organizational
variables which affect the number of innovations adopted are not
the same as those variables which affect innovation adoption as
a percentage of total decisions made, with the one exception of
number of potential choices available. In particular, decentralization which had a substantial impact on the innovation mean
had no significant effect on the percent innovation mean. Implicit in this finding is the notion that a main source of the substantial impact of decentralization on innovation means is the

117

increase in total number of organizational decisions made by
highly decentralized bureaus rather than any dramatic increase in
the success rate of innovation adoption, relative to the decision
universe.

Attempted innovations are defined in the innovation model as
unsuccessful innovations trials. With some exceptions, we found
that the organizational variables affecting the number of
attempted innovations were generally the same as those variables
affecting the number of innovations. This finding provides
support for the notion of a relatively constant success rate for
innovation adoptions vis-a-vis the more inclusive set of innovations attempts, both successful and unsuccessful. However, we
found that the number of innovations successfully adopted consistently exceeds the number of innovations which failed, for most
types of organizations. This finding acknowledges that innovation-
promoting managers may incur higher amounts of attempted innovation as well as higher amounts of innovation than non-innovation-
promoting managers; nonetheless, we have pointed out that the
excess of the latter over the former may somewhat ease the psychological pain of failure.

Organizational resource accumulation was found to have little
relation to organizational innovativeness. Rather, large amounts
of total bureau resources tended to be more closely related to
agency size and age. Big organizations from the standpoint of
large numbers of personnel and old organizations were generally
able to accumulate more resources than smaller younger agencies.
Seemingly, the "rich get richer" adage applies to organizations as
well as individuals. Such a finding would be exhilerating were we
concerned primarily with private sector organizations. Private
managers wishing to accumulate significant resources would promote
organizational growth and allow time to take its course. In the
public sector, however, the primary goal of public agencies from
the viewpoint of the citizen consumer should not be significant
resource accumulation. Many political campaigns and administrative careers have been made or broken on the issue of profligate
big government spending and misallocation of tax dollars. Citizens
are more concerned with the quality of government services than
public agencies growing old, "fat", and powerful. Public agency
resource acquisition is justifiable only when such an accumulation
is necessary to achieve organizational goals mandated legisla-
tively, and when the accumulation does not violate national policy
priority rankings.

In order to control for varying numbers or organizational
members, we looked at the impact of our independent variables on
dependent variable per capita means. Our findings about the
impact of our independent variables on per capita innovation and
attempted innovation means are generally the same as our findings

about the impact of these independent variables on the numbers of
innovation and attempted innovation incurred, although the per
capita means were somewhat more sensitive to the differential
effects of the organizational variables. In the case of bureau
resources, several organizational variables had the reverse effect
on per capita bureau resources. The effect of the variable on
total bureau resources was for the variable level presumed to be
less innovation-promoting to result in higher amounts of total
bureau resources; the effect of the variable on per capita bureau
resources was for the variable level presumed to be more
innovative-promoting to result in higher amounts of per capita
resources. Except for organizational age, when controlled for
the confounding effects of varying organizational size, innovation-
promoting factors result in higher per capita resources than non-
innovation-promoting factors. If per capita resource accumulation
can be viewed as a measure of efficiency, as might be argued since
organizational resources were initially determined in the innovation model on a per capita basis, organizations with innovation-
promoting structures are more efficient than organizations with
non-innovation-promoting structures.

Finally, we examined rates of change in our dependent variables. The striking fact about innovation and attempted innovation rates of change is the low values incurred for most types of
organizations tested. An eyeballing of the cumulative period
means shows that no organization substantially innovates or
attempts to innovate past its infancy, which may be defined as
five time periods, or five years. This rapid diminuition in
innovations adopted may occur because organizations rapidly seek
out the most favorable benefit-cost ratio in the range of potential ratios. Until technology developments alter the benefit-
cost ratio range, further innovation is not beneficial. The fact
that individual organizational members may become increasingly
less dissatisfied with the status quo as their suggestions are
accepted may also result in a reduction in the number of innovations adopted. There is no reason to believe that organizational
variable levels presumed to be innovation-promoting necessarily
result in higher rates of innovation or attempted innovation
change than non-innovation-promoting organizational variable
levels. In the case of organizational resource rates of change,
half of the variable levels presumed to be innovation-promoting
result in higher rates of change. The impact of organizational
variables on resource rates of change is somewhat greater than
the impact on innovation and attempted innovation rates of change.

The major implication of the rates of change findings, and
indeed, of the whole model, is that bureaucratic organizations of
all structural varieties do not innovate or attempt to innovate
for a very long period of time. The most likely organization to
innovate is a short-lived, highly decentralized agency which has
an unrestricted choice space. Perhaps we should take proposals

119

to systematically reformulate government agencies from the ground
up more seriously. To the extent that we wish our government
agencies to be innovative and to take fresh approaches to societal
problems, the coming ad-hocracy may, indeed, be the organization
of the future, as Toffler predicts.[2] Toffler describes the beginning of this trend toward temporary collegial administration as
project or task force management. Unlike the bureaucracy, the
task force is designed to be temporary. Toffler links the rise of
ad-hocracy to an increasingly frenzied rate of change in the
organizational environment. A relatively stable society presents
primarily routine and predictable problems to men. As societal
change is augmented, traditional forms of organization prove
inadequate to cope with the increased demands. Organizational
redesign becomes an on-going continuing function, as new technology and new management techniques place a totally flexible organization, alive with intelligence, information, and productive
capacity almost within our grasp.[3]

If the predictions of Toffler and the logical conclusions of
our innovation model are carried out, who will do the fundamental
work traditionally carried out by bureaucrats--i.e. the nitty
gritty work of daily routine administration? While routine work
will always call for some one-time decisions, much of this type of
endeavor is being automated and computerized. Permanency has been
a fundamental principle of Weberian bureaucracy. The concept of
an adhocracy government does not attack the principle of permanency, but rather the level at which permanency should occur. As
a result of our innovation model findings, we might argue that
permanency should be a tenet of government as a whole, rather than
any particular agency or department within government. By
increasing flexibility of government organization and ease of
movement of personnel, we may increase the probability that our
government agencies will focus today's resources on today's
problems as well as planning for the future, rather than continuing to pursue policies addressing the ills of yesteryear.

Footnotes, Chapter Seven:

[1]Chester I. Bernard, The Functions of the Executive
(Cambridge, Massachusetts: Harvard University Press, 2nd edition,
1968), p. 217.

[2]Alvin Toffler, Future Shock (New York, New York: Random
House, 1971), pp. 124-151.

[3]Ibid., pp. 135-136.

BIBLIOGRAPHY

Apter, Michael J. The Computer Simulation of Behavior (London: Hutchinson & Co., Ltd., 1970).

Argyris, Chris. "Some Limits of Rational Man Organizational Theory," Public Administration Review, Vol. 33, No. 3, (May-June 1973).

Bachrach, Peter and Morton S. Baratz, Power and Poverty: Theory and Practice (New York: Oxford University Press, 1970).

Becker, Selwyn W. and Thomas L. Whisler, "The Innovative Organization: A Selective View of Current Theory and Research," The Journal of Business, Vol. 40, No. 4, October 1967.

Bernard, Chester I. The Functions of the Executive (Cambridge, Massachusetts: Harvard University Press, 2nd edition, 1968).

Chiang, Alpha C. Fundamental Methods of Mathematical Economics (New York: McGraw-Hill, Inc., 1967).

Cohen, Michael D., James G. March, and Johan P. Olsen, "A Garbage Can Model of Organizational Choice," Administrative Science Quarterly, Vol. 17 (March 1972).

Cook, W. D., M. J. L. Kirby, and S. L. Mehndiretta, "A Linear Fractional Max-Min Problem," Operations Research, Vol. 23, No. 3 (May-June 1975).

Corwin, Ronald G. "Strategies for Organizational Innovation: An Empirical Conclusion," American Sociological Review, Vol. 37, No. 4 (August 1972).

Dresang, Dennis L. "Entrepreneurialism and Development Administration," Administrative Science Quarterly, Vol. 18, No. 1 (March 1973).

Downs, Anthony. Inside Bureaucracy (Boston: Little, Brown and Company, 1967).

Eitzen, D. Stanley and Norman R. Yetman, "Managerial Change, Longevity, and Organizational Effectiveness," Administrative Science Quarterly, Vol. 17, No. 1 (March 1972).

Etzioni, Amitai, Modern Organizations (Englewood Cliffs, N.J.: Prentice-Hall, Inc., 1964.

121

Etzioni, Amitai, "Mixed Scanning: A Third Approach to Decision-Making," Public Administration Review, Vol. 27, No. 5 (December 1967).

Fishman, George S. Concepts and Methods in Discrete Event Digital Simulation (John Wiley and Sons, Inc., 1973).

Francis, Wayne L. "Simulation of Committee Decision-Making in a State Legislative Body," Simulation and Games, Vol. 1, No. 3 (September 1970).

Frank, Andrew Gender, "Administrative Role Definition and Social Change," Human Organization, Vol. 22, No. 4 (Winter 1963-64).

Frijda, Nico H. "Problems of Computer Simulation," Computer Simulation of Human Behavior, eds. John M. Dutton and William H. Starbuck (New York: John Wiley and Sons, Inc., 1971).

Gullahorn, Jeane E. and John T., "Simulation and Social Science Theory: The State of the Union," Simulation and Games, Vol. 1, No. 1 (March 1970).

Gullahorn, Jeane E. and John T., "Some Computer Applications in Social Sciences," American Sociological Review, Vol. 30, No. 3 (June 1965).

Hage, Jerald and Michael Aiken, "Program Change and Organizational Properties: A Comparative Analysis," American Journal of Sociology, Vol. 72 (March 1967).

Helmich, Donald L. and Warren B. Brown, "Successor Types and Organizational Change in the Corporate Enterprise," Administrative Science Quarterly, Vol. 17, No. 3 (September 1972).

Kaufman, Herbert, The Limits of Organizational Change (University of Alabama Press, 1971).

Lambright, W. Henry, "Government and Technological Innovation: Weather Modification as a Case in Point," Public Administration Review, Vol. 32, No. 1 (Jan.-Feb. 1972).

Lindblom, Charles E. "The Science of Muddling Through," Public Administation Review, Vol. 29 (Spring 1959).

Maisel, Herbert and Giuliano Gnuglino, Simulations of Discrete Stochastic Systems (Science Research Associates, Inc., 1972).

Manser, Marilyn E., Thomas H. Naylor and Kenneth L. Wetz, "Effects of Alternative Policies for Allocating Federal Aid for Education to the States," Simulation and Games, Vol. 1, No. 2 (June 1970).

March, James G. and Herbert A. Simon, _Organizations_ (New York: John Wiley and Sons, Inc., 1958).

Marsten, R. E., W. W. Hogan, and J. W. Blankenship, "The Boxstep Method for Large-Scale Optimization," _Operations Research_, Vol. 23, No. 3 (May-June, 1975).

McClelland, David C., _The Achievement Motive_ (New York: Appleton-Century-Crofts, Inc., 1953).

McClelland, David C., _The Achieving Society_ (Princeton, N.J.: D. Van Nostrand Co., Inc., 1961).

McConnell, Grant. _Private Power and American Democracy_ (New York: Alfred A. Knopf, 1966).

McEachern, A. W., ed. "The Juvenile Probation Simulation: Simulation for Research and Decision-Making," _American Behavioral Scientist_, Vol. 11, No. 3 (Jan.-Feb. 1968).

McMahon, Graham and Michael Florian, "On Scheduling with Ready Times and Due Dates to Minimize Maximum Lateness," _Operations Research_, Vol. 23, No. 3 (May-June 1975).

Miller, James R. III, and Mason Haire, "Manplan: A Micro-Simulator for Manpower Planning," _Behavioral Science_, Vol. 15 (November 1970).

Mohr, Lawrence B., "Determinants of Innovation in Organization," _American Political Science Review_, Vol. 63, No. 1 (March 1969).

Mueller, Willard F. "A Case Study of Product Discovery and Innovation Costs," _Southern Economic Journal_, Vol. 24, No. 1 (July 1957).

Pool, Ithiel de Sola, Robert P. Abelson, and Sammuel L. Poplin, "A Postscript on the 1964 Election," _American Behavioral Scientist_, Vol. 8, No. 8 (April 1965).

Pool, Ithiel de Sola and Allan Kessler, "The Kaiser, the Tsar, and the Computer: Information Processing in a Crisis," _American Behavioral Scientist_, Vol. 8, No. 8 (April 1968).

Reitman, Julian, _Computer Simulation Applications_ (New York: John Wiley and Sons, Inc., 1971).

Rowe, Lloyd A. and William B. Boise, "Organizational Innovation: Current Research and Evolving Concepts," _Public Administration Review_, Vol. 34, No. 3 (May-June 1974).

Samuelson, Paul. Economics: An Introductory Analysis (New York: McGraw-Hill, Inc., 1967).

Schechter, Mordechai, "On the Use of Computer Simulation for Research," Simulation and Games, Vol. 2, No. 1 (March 1971).

Shapiro, Michael J., "The House and the Federal Role: A Computer Simulation of Roll-Call Voting," American Political Science Review, Vol. 62, No. 2 (June 1968).

Sharkansky, Ira, Public Administration: Policy Making in Government Agencies (Chicago: Markham Publishing Co., 1970).

Shepard, Herbert A., "Innovation-Resisting and Innovation Producing Organizations," The Journal of Business, Vol. 40, No. 4 (October 1967).

Sidman, Murray, "Operant Techniques," Experimental Foundations of Clinical Psychology, ed. Arthur J. Bachrach (New York: Basic Books, Inc. 1962).

Slevin, Dennis P. "The Innovation Boundary: A Replication with Increased Costs," Administrative Science Quarterly, Vol. 18, No. 1 (March 1973).

Smith, John. Computer Simulation Models (New York: Hafner Publishing Co., 1968).

Stein, Harold, Public Administration and Policy Development (New York: Harcourt, Brace, and World, Inc., 1952).

Strupp, Hanse H. "Patient-Doctor Relationships: Psychotherapist in the Therapeutic Process," Experimental Foundations of Clinical Psychology, ed. Arthur J. Bachrach (New York: Basic Books, Inc. 1962).

Thompson, Victor A. Bureaucracy and Innovation (University of Alabama Press, 1969).

Toffler, Alvin. Future Shock (New York, New York: Random House, 1971).

Watson, Donald Stevenson, Price Theory and Its Uses (Boston: Houghton Mifflin Co., 1968).

Whitney, Frederick L., The Elements of Research (New York: Prentice-Hall, Inc., 1950).

Zaltman, Gerald, Robert Duncan and Johnny Holbek, Innovations and Organizations (New York: John Wiley and Sons, 1973).

Zimmerman, H. J. and M. A. Pllatschek, "The Probability Distribu-
    tion Function of the Optimum of a 0-1 Linear Program with
    Randomly Distributed Coefficients of the Objective Function
    and the Right-Hand Side," Operations Research, Vol. 23,
    No. 1 (Jan.-Feb 1975).

APPENDIX

Following is a listing of the computer program which develops the innovation model simulation.

```
% THIS PROGRAM IS AN ORGANIZATIONAL SIMULATION.  THE PURPOSE OF THE
% SIMULATION IS TO VARY INPUT PARAMETERS AND TO DISCOVER THE IMPACT OF
% THIS VARIANCE, IF ANY, ON THE DEPENDENT VARIABLES.  IN PARTICULAR,
% THIS SIMULATION LOOKS AT THE IMPACT OF ORGANIZATIONAL CHARACTERISTICS
% ON ORGANIZATIONAL INNOVATION.
%
% LEVEL IS THE NUMBER OF LEVELS IN THE ORGANIZATION
% INUM IS THE NUMBER OF INDIVIDUALS IN THE ORGANIZATION
%
% ORES IS THE TOTAL AMOUNT OF ORGANIZATIONAL RESOURCES
%
% OSLAC IS THE AMOUNT OF ORGANIZATIONAL RESOURCES NOT COMMITTED TO FUTURE
% USES HENCE THE TOTAL AMOUNT OF ORGANIZATIONAL RESOURCES AVAILABLE FOR
% EXPERIMENTATION AND EXPLORATION OF INNOVATIVE CHOICES
%
% PSLAC IS THE PERCENTAGE OF TOTAL ORGANIZATIONAL RESOURCES WHICH IS SLACK
%
% PROB IS THE PROBABILITY OF A SUPERIOR CONSIDERING A SUBORDINATES
% SUGGESTION
%
% DECEN IS THE DEGREE OF DECENTRALIZATION IN AN ORGANIZATION; THAT IS, THE
% NUMBER OF THE LEVEL TO WHICH A CHOICE MUST PASS BEFORE ORGANIZATIONAL
% RESOURCES CAN BE EFFECTIVELY COMMITTED IN THE DECISION PROCESS
%
% VAR IS SOME INTEGER
% TEST IS SOME INTEGER
%
% IDIS1, IDIS2, AND IDIS3 ARE THREE ARRAYS, THE NUMBER OF SUBSCRIPTS OF
% EACH EQUALING THE NUMBER OF INDIVIDUALS IN THE ORGANIZATION.  IDIS IS A
% SIMILAR ARRAY.  FOR EACH INDIVIDUAL IDIS IS AN AGGREGATE OF IDIS1, THE
% RANDOM COMPONENT OF THE ITH INDIVIDUALHS DISSATISFACTION WITH THE STATUS
% QUO, IDIS2, THE COMPONENT ATTRIBUTABLE TO WHETHER OR NOT THE ITH
```

```
% INDIVIDUALS'S RECOMMENDATION WAS ATTEMPTED IN THE PREVIOUS FOUR TIME PERIODS
% AND IDIS3, THE COMPONENT REFLECTING WHETHER THE ITH INDIVIDUAL'S RECOMMENDATION
% OF ONE OF THE PREVIOUS FOUR TIME PERIODS WAS SUCCESSFULLY ADOPTED BY THE
% ORGANIZATION.
%
%. PINNOV IS THE PERCENTAGE OF ORGANIZATIONAL DECISIONS WHICH ARE SUCCESSFULLY
% ADOPTED INNOVATIONS.
%
% PERIOD IS AN ARRAY WITH SUBSCRIPTS EQUAL TO THE NUMBER OF TIME PERIODS
% IN ANY GIVEN RUN.
% IPOS IS THE INDIVIDUAL'S POSITION NUMBER IN THE ORGANIZATION
%
% IPOSN IS THE WITHIN LEVEL POSITION NUMBER OF THE ITH INDIVIDUAL
%
% ILEV IS THE LEVEL IN WHICH THE ITH INDIVIDUAL IS LOCATED
% IRES  THE AMOUNT OF RESOURCES AVAILABLE TO THE ITH INDIVIDUAL TO USE
% EXPLORING FOR INNOVATIVE CHOICES.
%
% CNUM IS THE MAXIMUM NUMBER OF CHOICES POTENTIALLY AVAILABLE TO THE ITH
% INDIVIDUAL
% CRISK IS THE CHOICE RISK FACTOR
% CFC IS THE CHOICE FIXED COST
% CPOS IS THE CHOICE POSITION OR IDENTIFICATION NUMBER
% CPO IS THE CHOICE PAYOFF
% CBCR IS THE CHOICE BENEFIT COST RATIO
%
% CTC IS THE CHOICE TOTAL COST
% RAN IS SOME RANDOM NUMBER
% RCBCR IS THE RECOMMENDED CHOICE BENEFIT COST RATIO
%
% SPAN IS THE SPAN OF CONTROL
%
```

129

% TEXAM IS THE NUMBER OF CHOICES AN INDIVIDUAL CAN EXAMINE IN A GIVEN TIME
% PERIOD.
%
% TRISK IS THE INDIVIDUAL'S RISK FACTOR
%
% IREC1 IS THE RECOMMENDATION OF THE ITHF INDIVIDUAL IS THE LAST TIME PERIOD
% IREC2 IS THE RECOMMENDATION OF THE ITH INDIVIDUAL 2 TIME PERIODS AGO
% IREC3 IS THE RECOMMENDATION OF THE ITHE INDIVIDUAL 3 TIME PERIODS AGO
% IREC4 IS THE RECOMMENDATION OF THE IH INDIVIDUAL 4 TIME PERIODS AGO
%
% SUB IS AN ARRAY CONSISTING OF THE POSITION NUMBERS OF AN INDIVIDUAL's
% SUBORDINATES.
%
% ADD IS SOME NUMBER
%
% SUM IS SOME NUMBER
%
% INNOV IS THE NUMBER OF INNOVATIONS UNDERTAKEN SUCCESSFULLY BY THE ORGAN
% ZATION UP THROUGH ANY GIVEN TIME PERIOD IN ANY GIVEN RUN.
%
% AINNOV IS THE NUMBER OF INNOVATIONS ATTEMPTED BY THE ORGANIZATION UP
% THROUGH ANY GIVEN TIME PERIOD IN ANY GIVEN RUN.
%
% DEC IS THE NUMBER OF DECISIONS MADE BY THE ORGANIZATION UP THROUGH ANY
% GIVEN TIME PERIOD IN ANY GIVEN RUN.
%
% IRRISK IS THE RISK FACTOR OF THE CHOICE RECOMMENDED BY THE ITH INDIVIDUAL IN
% ANY GIVEN TIME PERIOD.
%
% TPER IS THE TOTAL NUMBER OF TIME PERIODS IN ANY RUN.
%
% PER IS AN ARRAY WHOSE ELEMENTS CONSIST OF THE NUMBER OF TIME PERIODS

130

% TRANSPIRING IN A RUN UP TO ANY GIVEN POINT.
%

% P AFTER CERTAIN VARIABLES INDICATES AN ARRAY WHERE THE VALUE OF THAT
% VARIABLE IS GIVEN FOR EACH TIME PERIOD IN THE RUN
%

% M IN FRONT OF A VARIABLE INDICATES A MULTIPLYING FACTOR FOR THE VARIABLE
% IN QUESTION
%

% S IN FRONT OF A VARIABLE DENOTES A NUMBER TO BE SUBTRACTED FROM THE
% VARIABLE IN QUESTION
%

% A IN FRONT OF A VARIABLE DENOTES A NUMBER TO BE ADDED TO THE VARIABLE
% IN QUESTION
%

% REWARD INDICATES WHETHER OR NOT INDIVIDUALS ARE REWARDED FOR SUCCESSFUL
% INNOVATIONS 0=NO REWARDS FOR ANYONE 1=ANYONE RECOMMENDING A SUCCESSFUL
% INNOVATION IN THE LAST 4 TIME PERIODS RECEIVES AREW RESOURCE UNITS AT
% LEAST; ANY REMAINING RESOURCE UNITS ARE DISTRIBUTED RANDOMLY.
%

% PENALT INDICATES WHETHER OR NOT INDIVIDUALS ARE PENALIZED FOR UNSUCCES
% INNOVATIONS 0= NO PENALTIES FOR ANYONE; 1= ANYONE RECOMMENDING IN THE
% 4 TIME PERIODS AN UNSUCCESSFUL INNOVATION GETS PENALIZED SPEN RESOURCE UNITS
%

% KICK=1 KICKS THE PROGRAM OUT OF THE PENALTY LOOP
%

% INDUST IS THE PERCENTAGE OF CHOICES WHICH ARE REPLACED EVERY TIME
% PERIOD IS THE RATE OF INNOVATION OCCURRING IN THE INDUSTRY OR POLICY
% REPLAC IS THE ACTUAL NUMBER OF CHOICES REPLACED RANDOMLY EVERY TIME PERIOD
%

% STRISK IS THE AMOUNT SUBTRACTED FROM AN INDIVIDUAL'S RISK FACTOR IF HE
% RECOMMENDED AN UNSUCCESSFUL INNOVATION
%

131

```
%  AIRISK IS THE AMOUNT ADDED TO AN INDIVIDUAL'S RISK FACTOR IF HE HAS RECOMMENDED
%  A SUCCESSFUL INNOVATION
%
      INTEGER VAR,TEST,IDIS1(275),IDIS2(275),IDIS3(275)
      REAL PINNOV,PSLAC
      INTEGER LEVEL, INUM,ORES,OSLAC,PROB,DECEN
      INTEGER TPER, PER(40)
      INTEGER IPOS(275),ILEV(275),IRES(275)
      REAL CBCR(50),RCBCR(275)
      INTEGER SPAN
      REAL X(275)
      INTEGER CNUM,CRISK(50),CEC(50),CPO(50),CPOS(50),CTC(50)
      INTEGER IDIS(275),IRISK(275),IEXAM(275),IRC1(275)
      INTEGER IRC2(275),IRC3(275)
      INTEGER IRC4(275),SUB,SUM,INNOV,AINNOV,DEC
      REAL MCTC,MCFC,MCPO
      INTEGER TRRISK(275)
      INTEGER OSLACP(40),ORESP(40),DFCP(40),AINOVP(40),INNOVP(40)
      REAL PINOVP(40)
      REAL MIRISK,MIRES,DIVIDE,MIDIS1,MIDIS2,MIDIS3,SIDIS2,SIDIS3
      REAL REWARD,AREW,PENALT,SPEN
      INTEGER KICK
      REAL SIRICK,AIRISK,INDUST,MCRISK
      INTEGER REPLAC
      INTEGER BEE
%
%  THE NEXT STATEMENT READS IN VALUES FOR INPUT PARAMETERS.
      DO 2000 IJK = 1,15
      READ (11,850) SPAN,LEVEL,DECEN,TPER
850   FORMAT(13)
      READ (11,850) PROB,CNUM
      READ (11,600) PSLAC
```

132

```
600 FORMAT(F4.1)
    READ (11,600) MCTC,MCPO,MCFC
    READ (11,600) MIRISK,MIRES,DIVIDE,MIDIS1
    READ (11,600) MIDIS2,MIDIS3,SIDIS2,SIDIS3
    READ (11,600) REWARD,AREW,PENALT,SPEN
    READ (11,600) MCRISK,SIRISK,AIRISK
    READ (11,600) INDUST

IIREW=REWARD
IIPENA=PENALT
%
% THE FOLLOWING STATEMENT READS IN SEEDS FOR RANDU
    READ(10,851) X(1)
851 FORMAT(F9.0)
    WRITE(6,4999)
4999 FORMAT(' ','SEED=')
    WRITE(6,50000) X(1)
5000 FORMAT(' ',F9.0)
    KICK=0
%
% THIS LOOP FINDS THE TOTAL # OF INDIVIDUALS IN THE ORGANIZATION FOR THIS RUN
    INUM=0
    DO 1 I=1,LEVEL
    SUM=SPAN**(I-1)
1   INUM=INUM+SUM
    WRITE(6,900)
900 FORMAT(' ','INUM')
    WRITE(6,901) INUM
901 FORMAT(' ',I6)
%
% LOOP 3 DEFINES THE LEVEL OF THE INDIVIDUAL IN THE ORGANIZATION
    TEST=1
    SUM=0
```

133

```
      DO 4 J=1,LEVEL
      SUM=SPAN**(J-1) + SUM
    3 I=TEST,SUM
      ILEV(I)=J
    4 TEST=SUM+1
      WRITE(6,902)
  902 FORMAT(' ',' ILEV')
      WRITE(6,903) (I,ILEV(I),I=1,INUM)
  903 FORMAT(' ',5(I4,2X,I6))
%
%
%
%
%
%   THE NEXT STATEMENTS SET THE DEPENDENT VARIABLES EQUAL TO ZERO INITIAL
      PINNOV=0
      INNOV=0
      DEC=0
      AINNOV=0
%
%   IN LOOP 6 EACH PERSON IS RANDOMLY GIVEN A VALUE BETWEEN 1 & 10 TO INDI
%   CATE HIS OR HER DISSATISFACTION LEVEL.
%   EACH PERSON IS ALSO GIVEN A 1 TO 10 VALUE REPRESENTING WILLINGNESS TO
%   TAKE RISKS
      CALL RANDU(X,INUM)
      DO 6 I=1,INUM
      IPOS(I)=I
    6 IDIS(I)=MIDIS1*X(I)
      X(1)=X(INUM)*MIDIS1
      CALL RANDU(X,INUM)
      DO 30 I=1,INUM
      IRISK(I)=MIRISK**X(I)
```

134

```
%  THESE STATEMENTS INITIALIZE PREVIOUS RECOMMENDATION VARIABLES AT O.
       IRC4(I)=0
       IRC3(I)=0
       IRC2(I)=0
       IRC1(I)=0
%  THESE STATEMENTS INITIALLY SET EACH OF THE THREE COMPONENTS OF
%  THE DISSATISFACTION MEASURE = TO THE AVERAGE DISSATISFACTION MEASURE
       IDIS1(I)=IDIS(I)
       IDIS2(I)=IDIS(I)
   30  IDIS3(I)=IDIS(I)
       X(1)=X(INUM)*MIRISK
       WRITE(6,904)
  904  FORMAT(' ',' IPOS')
       WRITE(6,905)  (I,IPOS(I),I=1,INUM)
  905  FORMAT(' ',5(I4,2X,I6)
       WRITE(6,560)
  560  FORMAT(' ',' ITISK')
       WRITE(6,561)  (I,IRISK(I),I=1,INUM)
  561  FORMAT(' ',5(I4,2X,I6))
       WRITE(6,906)
  906  FORMAT(' ',' IDIS')
       WRITE(6,907)  (I,IDIS(I),I=1,INUM)
  907  FORMAT(' ',5(I4,2X,I6))
%
%  LOOP 7 RANDOMLY DISTRIBUTES RESOURCE TO INDIVIDUALS.
       CALL RANDU(X,INUM)
       DO 7 I=1,INUM
    7  IRES(I)=MIRES*X(I)
       X(1)=X(INUM)*MIRES
       WRITE(6,908)
  908  FORMAT(' ',' IRES')
       WRITE(6,909)  (I,IRES(I),I=1,INUM)
```

```
 909 FORMAT(' ',5(I4,2X,I6))
%
% LOOP 8 DERIVES TOTAL ORGANIZATIONAL SLACK BY SUMMING UP SLACK RESOURCE
% PREVIOUSLY DISTRIBUTED TO INDIVIDUALS.
       OSLAC=0
       DO 8 I=1,INUM
       SUM=IRES(I)
     8 OSLAC=OSLAC+SUM
       WRITE(6,910)
 910 FORMAT(' ','OSLAC')
       WRITE(6,911) OSLAC
 911 FORMAT(' ',I10)
%
       ORES=(OSLAC*100)/PSLAC
       WRITE(6,912)
 912 FORMAT(' ','ORES')
       WRITE(6,913) ORES
 913 FORMAT(' ',I10)
%
% LOOP 9 DEFINES POSITION, RISK FACTOR, TOTAL COST, PAYOFF, & FIXED COST
% EACH CHOICE
       CALL RANDU(X,CNUM)
       DO 9 I-1,CNUM
       CPOS(I)=I
     9 CRISK(I)=MCRISK*X(I)
       X(1)=MCRISK*X(CNUM)
       CALL RANDU(X,CNUM)
       DO 31 I=1,CNUM
    31 CTC(I)=MCTC*X(I)
       X(1)=X(CNUM)*NCTC
       CALL RANDU(X,CNUM)
       DO 32 I=1,CNUM
       CPO(I)=MCPO*X(I)
```

```
 32   CFC(I)=MCFC*(CTC(J))
      X(1)=X(CNUM)*MCPO
      WRITE(6,914)
914   FORMAT(' ','CPOS')
        WRITE(6,915)  (I,CPOS(I),I=1,CNUM)
915   FORMAT(' ',5(I4,2X,I6))
      WRITE(6,916)
916   FORMAT(' ','CRISK')
      WRITE(6,917)  (T,CRISK(I),I=1,CNUM)
917   FORMAT(' ',5(I4,2X,I6))
      WRITE(6,918)
918   FORMAT(' ','CIC')
      WRITE(6,919)  (I,CIC(I),T=1,CNUM)
919   FORMAT(' ',5(I4,2X,TI0))
      WRITE(6,920)
920   FORMAT(' ','CPO')
      WRITE(6,921)  (I,CPO(I),T=1,CNUM)
921   FORMAT(' ',5(I4,2X,I10))
      WRITE(6,922)
922   FORMAT(' ','CFC')
      WRITE(6,923)  (I,CFC(I),I=1,CNUM)
923   FORMAT(' ',5(I4,2X,I10))
      WRITE(6,304)
304   FORMAT(' ','PER       ','DECP      ','AINOVP    ','INNOVP    ',%
      'PINOVP    ','ORESP     ','OSLACP')
      CTC(1)=100
      CFC(1)=25
      CPO(1)=75
% LOOP 90 IS A BIG LOOP REFLECTING OCCURENCES IN ONE TIME PERIOD.
      IF(CTC(1).EQ.CFC(1))  (CTC(1)=CTC(1)+1
      CBCR(1)=1.0*(CPO(1))/(CTC(1)-CFC(1))
      DO 460 I=1,INUM
      RCBR(I)=CBCR(1)
```

137

```
      IRRISK(I)=0
      IRC1(I)=1
      IRC2(I)=1
      IRC3(I)=1
      IRC4(I)=1
460   CONTINUE
      DO 90 K=1,TPER
%
% IN LOOP 10 EACH INDIVIDUAL EXAMINES HIS OWN RESOURCES AND DISSATISFACTION
% LEVEL AND DECIDES WHETHER OR NOT TO RECOMMEND AN INNOVATIVE ALTERNATIVE
% OR THE STATUS QUO
      DO 10 I=1,INUM
% HERE THE MAXIMUM # OF CHOICES A PERSON CAN POTENTIALLY LOOK AT IN THIS
% TIME PERIOD IS SET AT THE LESSER OF THAT PERSON'S RESOURCES OR DISSATI ON
      RCBCR(I)=CBCR(1)
      IRRISK(I)=0
      IF (IRES(I).GT.IDIS(I)) GO TO 101
      IEXAM(I)=IRES(I)
      GO TO 102
101   IEXAM(I)=IDIS(I)
102   IF (IEXAM(I).LE.CNUM) GO TO 700
      IEXAM(I)=CNUM
700   IKE = IEXAM(I)
      BEE=0
      IF (IKE.EQ.0) GO TO 470
%
% IN LOOP 11 EACH PERSON COMPARES J CHOICE BENEFIT-RATIOS.
      DO 11 J=1,IKE
400   CALL RANDU(X,3)
      TEST=(X(1)*100)/DIVIDE+1
      X(1)=(X(3)*100)/DIVIDE+1
      IF (TEST.GT.CNUM) GO TO 400
      IF (TEST.EQ.1) GO TO 400
```

138

```
      IF (TEST.EQ.0) GO TO 400
      IF (CTC(TEST).EQ.0) GO TO 400
      IF (CPO(TEST).GT.0) GO TO 104
      IF (TEST.LF.1.OR.TEST.GT. CNUM) GO TO 400
104 IF (CRISK(TEST).LE.IRISK(I)) GO TO 105
      GO TO 11
105 IF (CTC(TEST).LE.ORES) GO TO 106
      GO TO 11
106 CBCR(TEST)=1.0*(CPO(TEST))/CTC(TEST)
      IF (CBCR(1).LE. CBCR(TEST)) GO TO 107
      GO TO 11
455   IRC4(I)=IRC3(I)
      IRC3(I)=IRC2(I)
      IRC2(I)=IRC1(I)
      IRC1(I)=CPOS(TEST)
      IRRISK(I)=CRISK(TEST)
      RCBCR(I)=CBCR(TEST)
      BEE=1
  11 CONTINUE
470 IF(BEE.EQ.1) GO TO 10
      IRC4(I)=IRC3(I)
      IRC3(I)=IRC2(I)
      IRC2(I)=IRC1(I)
      IRC1(I)=CPOS(1)
10 CONTINUE
%
% IN LOOP 108 SUPERIORS MAY OR MAY NOT EXAMINE THE RECOMMENDATIONS OF THEIR
% SUBORDINATES.
      SUB=2
      SUM=SPAN**(LEVEL-1)
      VAR=INUM-SUM
      DO 108 I=1,VAR
      IF (I.GT.INUM) GO TO 108
```

139

```
      IF (SUB.GT.INUM) GO TO 108
322IF(ILEV(I).LT.ILEV(SUB)) GO TO 321
      SUB=SUB+1
      GO TO 322
321 CALL RANDU(X,SPAN)
      DO 12 J=1, SPAN
      TEST=(10*X(J))+1
      IF (TEST.GE.PROB) GO TO 12
      IF (IRRISK(I).GE.IRRISK(SUB)) GO TO 109
      GO TO 12
109IF(RCBCR(I).GE.RCBCR(SUB)) GO TO 12
      IRRISK(I)=IRRISK(SUB)
      RCBCR(I)=RCBCR(SUB)
      IRC1(I)=IRC1(SUB)
12 SUB=SUB+1
108 CONTINUE
      X(10=(X(SPAN)*10)+1
%
%
% LOOP 13 BEGINS THE PROCESS OF ORGANIZATIONAL DECISION MAKING.
      DO 13 I=1, INUM
% HERE WE LOOK FOR INDIVIDUALS WITH AUTHORITY TO MAKE ORGANIZATIONAL DECISIONS
      IF (ILEV(I).LE.DECEN) GO TO 110
      GO TO 13
110DEC=DEC+1
%
% HERE WE TEST TO SEE IF AN ATTEMPTED INNOVATION IS SUCCESSFULLY ADOPTED
      CALL RANDU (X,3)
      TEST=(10*X(1))+1
      X(1)=(X(3)*10)+1
%
% LOOP 14 READJUSTS DISSATISFACTION LEVELS FOR INDIVIDUALS PREVIOUSLY
% RECOMMENDING AN ATTEMPTED INNOVATION
```

```
      DO 14 J=1,INUM
      IF (IRC1(J).NE.IRC1(I)) GO TO 111
      IDIS2(J)=(IDIS2(J)-SIDIS2)*MIDIS2
      IRISK(J)=IRISK(J)-SIRISK
111IF(IRC2(J).NE.IRC1(I)) GO TO 112
      IDIS2(J)=IDIS2(J)-SIDIS2)*MIDIS2
      IRISK(J)=IRISK(J)-SIRISK
112IF(IRC3(J).NE.IRC1(I)) GO TO 113
      IDIS2(J)=(IDIS2(J)-SIDIS2)*MIDIS2
      IRISK(J)=IRISK(J)-SIRISK
113IF(IRC4(J).NF.IRC1(I)) GO TO 14
      IDIS2(J)=(IDIS2(J)-SIDIS2)*MIDIS2
      IRISK(J)=IRISK(J)-SIRISK
14    CONTINUE
      IF (IRC1(I).NE.1) GO TO 475
      ORES=ORES+CPO(1)-CTC(1)+CFC(1)
      OSLAC=ORES*PSLAC/100
      RINNOV=1.0*INNOV/DEC
      PER(K)=K
      ORESP(K)=ORES
      OSLACP(K)=OSLAC
      DECP(K)=DEC
      AINOVP(K)=AINNOV
      INNOVP(K)=INNOV
      PINOVOP(K)=PINNOV
      GO TO 310
475   IF (TEST.GT.IRISK(I) GO TO 114
      VAR=IRC1(I)
      AINNOV=AINNOV+1
      OSLAC=ORES*PSLAC/100
      PINNOV=1.0*INNOV/DEC
      PER(K)=K
      OSLACP(K)=OSLAC
```

```
          ORESP(K)=ORES
          DECP(K)=DEC
          AINOVP(K)=AINNOV
          INNOVP(K)=INNOV
          PINOVP(K)=PINNOV
          GO TO 310
114  VAR=IRC1(I)
     INNOV=INNOV+1
     PINNOV=FLOAT(INNOV)/FLOAT(DEC)
     ORES=ORES-CTC(VAR)+CPO(VAR)
     OSLAC=(ORES*PSLAC)/100
%
% THIS PUTS THE RECENTLY CHOSEN INNOVATION INTO CHOICE POSITION #1
     TEST=IRC1(I)
     CTC(1)=CTC(TEST)
     CFC(1)=CFC(TEST)
     CPO(1)=CPO(TEST)
     CBCR(1)=1.0*(CPO(TEST))/(CTC(TEST))
%
% THIS GENERATES A NEW CHOICE TO REPLACE THE SUCCESSFUL INNOVATION
     CALL RANDU(X,3)
     CRISK(TEST)=MCRISK*X(1)
     X(1)=X(3)*MCRISK
     CALL RANDU (X,3)
     CTC(TEST)=MCTC*X(1)
     X(1)=X(3)*MCTC
     CALL RANDU(X,3)
     CPO(TEST)=MCPO*X(1)
     CFC(TEST)=MCFC*(CTC(TEST))
     X(1)=X(3)*MCPO
%
% LOOP 80 READJUSTS DISSATISFACTION LEVELS FOR INDIVIDUALS RECOMMENDING A
% SUCCESSFULLY ADOPTED INNOVATION.
```

142

```
      DO 80 J=1,INUM
      IF (IRC1(J).NE.IRC1(I)) GO TO 115
      IDIS3(J)=(IDIS3(J)-SIDIS3)*MIDIS3
      IRISK(J)=IRISK(J)+ATRISK
115   IF(IRC2(J).NE.IRC1(I)) GO TO 116
      IDIS3(J)=(IDIS3(J)-SIDIS3)*MIDIS3
      IRISK(J)=IRISK(J)+AIRISK
116   IF(TRC3(J).NE.IRC1(I)) GO TO 117
      IDIS3(J)=(IDIS3(J)-SIDIS3)*MIDIS3
      IRISK(J)=TRISK(J)+AIRISK
117   IF(IRC4(J).NE.IRC1(I)) GO TO 80
      IDIS3(J)=(IDIS3(J)-SIDIS3)*MIDIS3
      IRISK(J)=IRISK(J)+AIRISK
80    CONTINUE
      PINNOV=1.0*INNOV/DEC
      PER(K)=K
      OSLACP(K)=OSLAC
      ORESP(K)=ORES
      DECP(K)=DEC
      AINOVP(K)=AINNOV
      INNOVP(K)=INNOV
      PINOVP(K)=PINNOV
%
% LOOP 16 RECOMPUTES DISSATISFACTION LEVELS FOR EACH INDIVIDUAL.
310   CALL RANDU(X,INUM)
      DO 16 J=1,INUM
      IDIS1(J)=MIDIS1*X(J)
      IDIS(J)=(IDIS1(J)+IDIS2(J)+IDIS3(J))/3
      IF (IDIS(J).GE.0) GO TO 16
      IDIS(J)=0
16    CONTINUE
      X(1)=X(INUM)*MIDIS1
%
```

143

```
% LOOP 300 REWARDS PERSONS FOR RECOMMENDING SUCCESSFUL INNOVATIONS.
  IF (TIREW.EQ.0) GO TO 17
     DO 300 J=1,TNUM
     IF (IRC1(J).EQ.IRC1(I)) GO TO 301
     IF (IRC2(J).EQ.IRC1(I)) GO TO 301
     IF (IRC3(J).EQ.IRC1(I)) GO TO 301
     IF (IRC4(J).EQ.TRC1(I)) GO TO 301
     GO TO 300
 301 IF (OSLAC.LT.AREW) GO TO 300
     IRES(J)=AREW
     OSLAC=OSLAC-AREW
 300 CONTINUE
%
% LOOP 18 REDISTRIBUTES RANDOMLY ORGANIZATIONAL SLACK TO INDIVIDUALS.
  17 CALL RANDU(X,TNUM)
     DO 18 J=1,TNUM
     TEST=(10*X(J))+1
     IF (TEST.LT.5) GO TO 118
     IF (OSLAC.GT.0) GO TO 18
     GO TO 19
 118 IRES(J)=IRES(J)+5
     OSLAC=OSLAC-5
     IF (OSLAC.GT.0) GO TO 18
     GO TO 315
  18 CONTINUE
%
% LOOP 302 PENALIZES PERSONS FOR RECOMMENDING UNSUCCESSFUL INNOVATIONS
 315 IF (TIPENA.EQ.0) GO TO 19
     IF (KICK.EQ.1) GO TO 19
     DO 302 J=1, INUM
  KICK=1
     IF (IRC1(J).EQ.IRC1(I)) GO TO 303
     IF (IRC2(J).EQ.IRC1(I)) GO TO 303
```

```
      IF (IRC3(J).EQ.IRC1(I)) GO TO 303
      IF (IRC4(J).EQ.IRC1(I)) GO TO 303
      GO TO 302
  303 IRES(J)=IRES(J)-SPEN
      IF (IRES(J).LT.0) IRES(J)=0
  302 CONTINUE
      IF (OSLAC.GT.0) GO TO 17
   19 CONTINUE
   13 CONTINUE
%
% THIS WRITES OUT THE OUTPUT OF THE SIMULATION
      WRITE(6,479) PER(K),DECP(K),AINOVP(K),INNOVP(K),PINOVP(K),%
      ORESP(K),OSLACP(K)
  479 FORMAT(' ',I3,'   ',I4,'    ',I6,'    ',I6,'    ',%
      F7.6,'  ',I5,'  ',I6)
%
% LOOP 538 REPLACES CHOICES RANDOMLY ACCORDING TO THE RATE OF INNOVATION IN THE
% POLICY AREA
      REPLAC=INDUST*CNUM
      IF (REPLAC.EQ.0) GO TO 90
      DO 538 J=1,REPLAC
      TEST=0
  334 CALL RANDU(X,3)
      TEST=(X(1)*100)/DIVIDE+1
      X(1)=(X(3)*100)/DIVIDE+1
      IF (TEST.LF.1) GO TO 334
      IF (TEST.GT.CNUM) GO TO 334
      CALL RANDU(X,3)
      CRISK(TEST)=MCRISK*X(1)
      X(1)=X(3)*MCRISK
      CALL RANDU(X,3)
      CTC(TEST)=MCTC*X(1)
      X(1)=X(3)*MCTC
```

145

```
        CALL RANDU(X,3)
        CPO(TEST)=MCPO*X(1)
        CFC(TEST)=MCFC*(CTC(TEST))
        X(1)=X(3)*MCPO
  538 CONTINUE
    %
   90 CONTINUE
    REWIND 11
    %
 2000CONTINUE
        STOP
        END
```

146